FLORIDA
FLASHPOINTS

EXTRAORDINARY MOMENTS
FROM SPANISH COLONY TO THE SPACE AGE

RANDY JAYE

THE
History
PRESS

Published by The History Press
Charleston, SC
www.historypress.com

First published 2025

Manufactured in the United States

ISBN 9781467155830

Library of Congress Control Number: 2024949762

Notice: The information in this book is true and complete to the best of our knowledge. It is offered without guarantee on the part of the author or The History Press. The author and The History Press disclaim all liability in connection with the use of this book.

CONTENTS

Spanish Missions in Florida...30
English Slave Raiding into Florida...31
The Apalachee Massacre 32
Collapse of the Spanish Missions in Florida 32
More Attacks from the North 33
Indians from the North Flee to Florida 33
European-Introduced Diseases, Warfare and Slavery.......................33
Today's Native Americans in Florida 35

5. Pensacola Founded..36
The Original Establishment of Pensacola in 1559.........................37
"Modern" Pensacola Established in 1698 40

6. St. Augustine Founded 42
The Establishment of St. Augustine in 1565 43
The Destruction of French Fort Caroline 43
The Matanzas Massacre of the French 45
St. Augustine's Endurance 46

7. Ranching and Cattle Heritage...................................47
Florida's Confederate "Cow Cavalry"....................................49
Florida's Modern Cattle Industry 50

8. Intricate Connections to Slavery...............................53
Black Seminoles 54
British Period (1763–83)..55
Second Spanish Period (1783–1821) 56
United States Rule (1821–61) 56
Slavery During the Confederacy (1861–65) 58
The End of Slavery in the United States 58

9. Fort Mose: Colonial America's First Free Black Town............59
Siege of St. Augustine (Battle of Bloody Mose) 59

10. The British Period (1763–83)..................................64
British East and West Florida 64
Kings Road 66
The American Revolutionary War (1775–83) 67

4

INTRODUCTION

In 1513, Spanish conquistador Juan Ponce de León landed in Florida, marking the beginning of the European invasion. Since then, empires (Spanish, French and English), many Indigenous tribes, Black slaves, freed slaves, escaped slaves and migrants from various parts of North America have settled in Florida.

Florida has been the focal point of many historic events, including several wars, disastrous hurricanes and the race to the moon during the Cold War, and has become the home of many world-class entertainment parks. These important events have not only shaped the state but also influenced the development and helped structure the identity and culture of the entire nation. However, many other important historic episodes, some little known, nearly unknown or forgotten, have occurred in Florida, including the establishment of the first European settlement in the present-day continental United States, the decimation of nearly all its original Indigenous peoples due to European incursions and diseases, the Matanzas Massacre (which squelched French plans to colonize Florida), the Patriot Rebellion (which led to other hostilities that reshaped the nation), the land boom and bust of the 1920s (a precursor to the Great Depression) and major election issues (two of which led to the seating of United States presidents).

This book explores the very roots of Florida as it traces the state's long history through many of its most interesting and consequential historic episodes. It also explores various remarkable turnarounds in terrain and policies, including the taming of dense swamps and thick woodlands to allow for commercial and agricultural enterprises and residential habitation in the Everglades, the civil rights battles to end Jim Crow racial segregation, Florida's political shift from a southern Democrat to a Republican stronghold state and a history altered multiple times by massive storms, mainly hurricanes.

This is not a textbook or an academic dissertation or thesis, as it is written in an informal format attractive to most people who do not want to be overwhelmed with an overabundance of notes and overemphasized details. So relax and prepare to take a fascinating journey through more than five hundred years of some of the most interesting historic events you may ever encounter.

CHAPTER 1

JUAN PONCE DE LEÓN CLAIMS LA FLORIDA FOR THE SPANISH EMPIRE

Florida was the first region in the present-day United States, and the North American mainland, to be permanently settled by Europeans. On April 2, 1513, the Spanish conquistador Juan Ponce de León spotted land that he believed was an island. The following day, he brought a landing party ashore somewhere in present-day northeastern Florida. Ponce de León claimed the land for the Spanish Empire and named it La Florida because its landscape had an abundance of flowers and it was the Easter season, which the Spanish called Pascua Florida (Festival of Flowers).

Geographically, La Florida became an undetermined Spanish territory that stretched from Newfoundland to the Florida Keys along North America's eastern coastline, but no western boundaries could be adequately defined, as they would remain unexplored and unknown to Europeans for many decades.

Contrary to popular belief, Ponce de León was not the first known European to set foot on the North American mainland. The earliest known substantiated evidence of Europeans traveling to the North American mainland dates to around 1000 AD, when the Viking explorer Leif Erikson led a crew sailing in a wooden ship, with an enormous single sail, landed on the northern tip of present-day Newfoundland, Canada. Erikson established a village at L'Anse aux Meadows, Newfoundland, that included eight buildings, which is now thought to have been a ship repair facility with iron-forging capabilities. The settlement turned out to be temporary, as it was abandoned after a decade. Archaeological and

Juan Ponce de León landing in La Florida in 1513. Painting by Don J. Emory. *Courtesy of the Halifax Historical Museum, Daytona Beach. Photograph by author.*

other scientific research confirmed the authenticity of the L'Anse aux Meadows settlement, and the remains of the Norse village are now part of a UNESCO World Heritage Site.

Another European, Italian navigator John Cabot, led expeditions under the commission of Henry VII, king of England, to the North American mainland in 1497 and 1498 and explored the eastern coast of present-day Canada.

Between 1509 and 1512, a ship commanded by Spanish explorer Diego de Miruelo, which was on a slave-raiding mission, was driven north by a storm from Lucayos (the present-day island group of the Bahamas and the

Turks and Caicos Islands). Diego de Miruelo's ship landed on territory that Ponce de León later named La Florida and made contact with Indigenous peoples. The news of previously unknown Indigenous settlements near Spanish territories in the Caribbean prompted other slave traders to raid the area prior to 1513.

THE "FABLED" EXPEDITION

Ponce de León, as well as many other mariners in the New World, were aware of unexplored land to the northwest of Hispaniola (present-day Haiti and the Dominican Republic) prior to 1513, but did not know how distant they were from established Spanish settlements in the Caribbean. The Indigenous people of the West Indies also told the Spanish stories of a legendary island to the north that they called Beniny (Bimini). The 1502 Cantino planisphere (world map), drawn by an unknown Portuguese cartographer, shows a peninsula-shaped land mass north of Cuba, which is most likely a depiction of Florida. Another curious map drawn by Peter Martyr d'Anghiera in 1511 depicts the Caribbean basin and actually includes the coastline that would be named La Florida two years later.

In February 1512, Ponce de León obtained a royal contract from the Spanish government to set out on a voyage of discovery in the New World. The contract stipulated that he was to search for gold and other items of value (with provisions for a percentage of the booty to be shared with the Spanish Empire) and that Native Indians were to be captured, enslaved and forced to work in mines in Spain's New World colonies. Additionally, any new lands discovered were to be claimed as colonial territory under the rule of the Spanish Empire, and Ponce de León was to be appointed governor for life of these new lands.

In 1513, Ponce de León used the fortune he gained from his plantations and mines in Puerto Rico to personally hire a crew of approximately two hundred men and purchase a small fleet of three ships, called the *Santiago*, the *San Cristobal* and the *Santa Maria de la Consolacio*.

On March 4, 1513, he set sail from Puerto Rico on his fabled journey of exploration in the New World. After voyaging northwest for twenty-three days, the crew sighted an unfamiliar island while sailing northwest of Lucayos. It has never been verified if this was their first sighting of the North American mainland or one of the northern present-day Bahama islands.

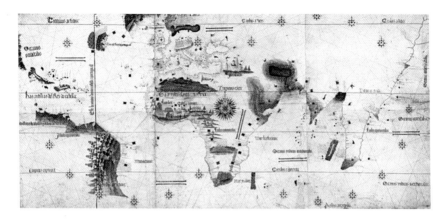

The Cantino Planisphere world map, circa 1502. Note the depiction of what appears to be the Florida peninsula above the island of Cuba (top left corner of the map). *Courtesy of Wikimedia Commons.*

Around noon on April 2, 1513, the crew sighted more unfamiliar land, which they believed to be another island. The expedition continued to sail northward, keeping the land in sight as they searched for a harbor. At nightfall, the fleet finally anchored in eight fathoms of water near the coastline, determined to explore this curious land.

THE CLAIMING AND CHRISTENING OF LA FLORIDA IN 1513

On the morning of April 3, 1513, Ponce de León led a landing party as they rowed ashore on longboats to this curious land that was flat and thick with subtropical vegetation and flowers. He christened this new "island" La Florida and claimed it for the Spanish Empire. Unknown to Ponce de León or any other European was the estimated 350,000 Indigenous people who were living in the Florida peninsula at that time.

There is no Plymouth Rock to identify the exact spot where this first officially documented Spanish landing came ashore on the North American mainland. Several historians have proposed theories attempting to identify the precise landing spot, which range from St. Augustine to Melbourne Beach and including some locations in between. Considering the navigation device (either a quadrant or a mariner's astrolabe) that was used to record the position in Ponce de León's logbook (which is now lost to history) and the changing of the coastline due to hurricanes and development over the many years since the landing, the precise spot will either remain controversial or, most likely, never be accurately identified.

Ponce de León remained and explored the area around his first landing site for five days. During this time, his logbook made no mention of coming in contact with any Indigenous people or discovering gold or other precious metals.

CONTINUED EXPLORATION OF LA FLORIDA

On April 8, 1513, Ponce de León's fleet pulled up their anchors, and the expedition sailed north along the coast of La Florida for one day. The following day, they reversed their course and sailed south for eleven days. They spotted an Indian settlement near the coastline, but after anchoring for the night, the fleet continued southward without going ashore to attempt to interact with the Native Indians at this location.

On May 4, 1513, the fleet reached and christened Biscayne Bay. They were forced to anchor for repairs at the island they christened Santa Marta (present-day Key Biscayne). A landing party went ashore and explored a Native Indian mound settlement. However, all the people of the Tequesta tribe in that area fled into the woods, which may have been an indication of a previous hostile interaction with European slavers.

On May 15, 1513, the fleet continued southward along a string of islands they christened Los Martires (the present-day Florida Keys).

On May 23, 1513, they reached the southwestern side of the Florida peninsula mainland and were encountered by Native Indians from the Calusa tribe, who chased them away after surrounding their ships in sea canoes full of warriors armed with bows and arrows. After sailing northward, Ponce de León was forced to anchor for a few days and repair the ships due to water leakage. A landing party encountered more Calusa Native Indians, and several armed clashes broke out; both sides suffered casualties. The Spanish managed to capture eight Calusa tribesmen and used one of them as a translator. Sign language, expressions and gestures were used to communicate.

On June 4, 1513, the fleet was attacked by more Calusa warriors in sea canoes near present-day Sanibel Island. The fleet retreated and sailed in search of more islands, which the captive Calusa warriors indicated were located close by.

On June 21, 1513, the fleet reached the present-day Dry Tortugas, where they obtained food supplies by hunting turtles, seals and seabirds. With replenished supplies, the fleet then attempted to return to Puerto Rico by sailing around Cuba but failed due to strong sea currents. The fleet then backtracked north to the east side of the Florida Keys and then further northward along La Florida's east coast.

On July 8, 1513, the fleet managed to find its way back to the familiar Grand Bahama Island, where Ponce de León disbanded the expedition that is credited for the Spanish discovery and christening of La Florida.

On October 19, 1513, Ponce de León returned to his home in Puerto Rico.

For several years after the discovery and christening of La Florida, the Spanish continued to believe it was an island. When Spanish conquistador and cartographer Alonso Álvarez de Pineda explored the Gulf of Mexico in 1519, his expedition determined that the La Florida peninsula was part of a large land mass.

THE FOUNTAIN OF YOUTH LEGEND

A popular legend states that while Juan Ponce de León was searching for the Fountain of Youth (a mythical spring with waters that restore youth to anyone who drinks from or bathes in them and gives everlasting life), he wound up discovering La Florida. Tales of a Fountain of Youth can be traced around the world for thousands of years before Ponce de León was born. There are no known documents associated with Ponce de León during his lifetime that even mention the Fountain of Youth. The story that attached Ponce de León to the search for the Fountain of Youth was actually created after his death. In 1535, fourteen years after Ponce de León's death, Gonzalo Fernández de Oviedo y Valdés (a Spanish court chronicler with intentions to discredit Ponce de León) wrote in his *Historia general y natural de las Indias* that Ponce de León was searching for the waters of Bimini to restore his youth.

To this day, the myth of Ponce de León's search for the magical Fountain of Youth remains one of the United States' greatest and most well-known legends. Florida's tourist industry capitalizes on the Fountain of Youth legend as visitors from all over the world strive to drink from the stone well at St. Augustine's Fountain of Youth Archaeological Park. This glamorized water actually comes from a 240-foot-deep well and is treated and certified as safe for human consumption by the City of St. Augustine.

JUAN PONCE DE LEÓN'S LEGACY

Today, Ponce de León is world famous for the Spanish discovery and christening of La Florida. Additionally, his first successful exploration of La Florida led to a wave of more expeditions that revealed the coastlines of the Gulf of Mexico, the eastern coast of the present-day United States, Mexico and the South American continent. After the Spanish empire claimed many of these lands and conquered many Indigenous peoples, including the Aztec and Inca civilizations, its colonial expansion transformed the entire world and made Spain one of the most prosperous global empires during the sixteenth, seventeenth and eighteenth centuries.

CHAPTER 2

THE NARVÁEZ EXPEDITION

On December 11, 1526, Pánfilo de Narváez was granted a license by King Charles V of Spain to lead an expedition to conquer Indigenous peoples, establish Spanish settlements and military garrisons and search for gold and other riches along the Gulf of Mexico in La Florida.

By 1527, the Narváez expedition (sometimes referred to as the Florida expedition) was well-funded and hopeful of success as it sailed from Spain with about six hundred people who originated in Spain, Portugal, Greece, Italy and Africa. After several hardships and delays, the expedition arrived in La Florida in April 1528.

It would be eight years before any information about the fate of the Narváez expedition's landing party would surface.

THE NARVÁEZ EXPEDITION LANDS IN LA FLORIDA IN 1528

On April 12, 1528, the Narváez expedition spotted land on La Florida's Gulf coast north of present-day Tampa Bay. The expedition's pilot, Diego de Miruelo, guided the fleet south for two days, searching for what he believed was a great harbor. One of the expedition's ships was lost during the search for this great harbor.

The Narváez expedition finally decided to anchor at Boca Ciega Bay (north of present-day Tampa Bay). Buildings set on top of earthen mounds belonging to the Indigenous people of the Safety Harbor Culture were

Pánfilo de Narváez was described as a man of authoritative personality with a boisterous voice, tall of body, somewhat blond and inclined to redness. *Courtesy of Wikimedia Commons.*

sighted, and the expedition's comptroller, Alonso Enríquez, went ashore at the present-day Jungle Prada Site in St. Petersburg with a small landing party, managing to trade items such as glass beads, brass bells and cloth for fresh fish and meat with the Native Americans.

Narváez then ordered a landing party of three hundred ashore to establish a camp. The expedition's Spanish officials declared Narváez the royal governor of La Florida. Spain's Requerimiento (Requirement) was read to the Native Americans, informing them of Spain's rights of conquest under God's plan. Narváez then informed the Native Americans that they had the choice to convert to Christianity and explained that they would be welcomed and loved if they did and conquered and enslaved if they did not. The Requerimiento and other demands were read to the Indigenous people in Spanish, so any who were listening surely had no understanding of the Spaniards' intentions of claiming their lands and forcing change to their religion and culture.

THE EXPEDITION DIVIDES INTO LAND AND SEA EXCURSIONS

On May 1, 1528, Narváez decided to split the expedition into land and sea excursions. He planned to lead a crew of three hundred over land northward while the ships and their crew of one hundred were to sail north and meet up at the mouth of Tampa Bay. This plan was foiled because the mouth of Tampa Bay was actually south. Due to Narváez's errors in strategy and geography, the land and sea crews never met again.

The land expedition found itself struggling to survive in La Florida's wilderness as many were injured, hungry and sick. Narváez suspected that some of the expedition's healthier men were considering desertion, and he became fearful that they might steal horses and ride away to find relief for themselves, away from their sick and starving companions. However, Cabeza de Vaca convinced the potential conspirators to remain with the expedition and in loyal service to the king of Spain.

On August 4, 1528, Narváez ordered his expedition to begin forging tools and building boats. During the effort to build the boats, one horse every three days was killed for food, and additional food, mainly corn, was pilfered from fields of the nearby Aute village. At least ten of Narváez's men were killed by Apalachee warriors while gathering shellfish during this time as well.

On September 20, 1528, five flat-bottomed boats thirty to forty feet long and capable of supporting a crew of about fifty people each were completed. However, these boats were of questionable seaworthiness.

On September 22, 1528, the expedition's 242 survivors set sail from a bay they named Bahia de los Caballos (Bay of Horses), present-day Apalachee Bay, in honor of their sacrificed horses.

JOURNEY TO TEXAS, THE SOUTHWEST AND MEXICO

Survival was now the goal of the expedition rather than conquest. The five boats sailed west along the coast of the Gulf of Mexico searching for any Spanish ships that could save them from their deadly and failed excursion into La Florida. Low on essential supplies and suffering from dehydration, men began dying off.

Strong winds violently churned the sea, and what was left of the expedition washed ashore on the east coast of present-day Texas. It was here, in 1529, that Narváez's boat drifted out to sea as most of his men were camped on shore. He was never seen again and was presumed drowned.

The boats now lost or unable to sail left the surviving men of Narváez's expedition castaways and spread out along the coast of Texas. Many were killed by local Indigenous warriors, and others were held captive by various tribes for several years as they struggled to survive. By the winter of 1534, there were only four survivors of Narváez's expedition. They managed to meet up and escape from their captors and flee to southwestern Texas, where they met other Indigenous people who were more hospitable.

By December 1535, the four survivors, Alonso del Castillo Maldonado, Andrés Dorantes de Carranza, Álvar Núñez Cabeza de Vaca and Estevanico, an enslaved Black Moor, had become the first known Europeans and African to cross the North American continent and were near the salty waters of the Gulf of California. They turned south and headed for Cortés's Mexico. After

The approximate route of the Narváez expedition (1527–36). *Courtesy of Wikimedia Commons.*

meeting an Indigenous man wearing a Spanish belt buckle as a necklace and being told that a Spanish outpost was nearby, their hopes of finally finding their way back to the world of Spanish domain were high.

The four survivors met many Indigenous people who had fled from Spanish slaving raids as they traveled through northern Mexico, where they found villages burned and abandoned.

In July 1536, near present-day Sinaloa, Mexico, the four survivors happened across a group of Spanish slavers. The four survivors were almost unrecognizable to the Spanish, as they were dressed in animal skins and accompanied by thirteen Indigenous people.

The four survivors were escorted to Mexico City by twenty armed cavalry troops and six slavers, who were driving about five hundred Indigenous people shackled in chains. They arrived there on July 23, 1536, and were treated as celebrities.

The Narváez expedition is one of the greatest epic stories of both failure and survival of all the European odysseys during the Age of Exploration. It enticed future Spanish expeditions into the mysterious regions of North America and La Florida, which remained under Spanish control for more than 250 years.

CHAPTER 3

HERNANDO DE SOTO'S EXPLORATION OF NORTH AMERICA

The purpose of Hernando de Soto's extensive four-year exploration of North America (1539–43) was to search for gold, locate areas to establish Spanish settlements and find a passage to China or the Pacific Coast.

In 1539, the expedition started in La Florida with more than six hundred crewmen and two hundred horses. It was the first known European expedition to venture into the interior of the present-day United States.

De Soto assumed that the Indigenous people inhabiting La Florida would be similar to the Inca people he encountered in Peru, who served as his guides and possessed and mined large quantities of gold and silver. However, he found that the Indigenous peoples of La Florida mistrusted the Spanish explorers, mainly due to previous hostile encounters with European slave raiders and the expeditions of Juan Ponce de León and Pánfilo de Narváez.

PLANNING FOR THE EXPLORATION

In 1537, the king of Spain appointed de Soto governor of Cuba and contracted him to lead the conquest of La Florida. De Soto was also appointed adelantado (the civil and military governor of a province in Spain or her colonies) of La Florida, which granted him the authority to govern all lands he conquered. The exploration was funded and organized by de Soto. His reputation as a successful conquistador of the Inca Empire and the perceived riches in North America assisted him in the recruitment of men and investors.

Engraving of Hernando de Soto. *Courtesy of Wikimedia Commons.*

Information about La Florida in the 1530s was scarce: only a few inaccurate maps existed, and none included any details of the interior regions of the territory. De Soto was fascinated by the stories of Cabeza de Vaca, who was one of the four survivors of the Narváez expedition's eight-year journey through La Florida and parts of North America. The fact that only four men from the expedition survived the arduous journey through the mysterious lands of La Florida encouraged de Soto to organize a larger entrada with greater military and material resources.

By the beginning of 1538, de Soto had acquired nine ships, a crew of over six hundred men (Spanish, Portuguese and Atlantic Creoles of mixed-race African descent), hundreds of weapons and pieces of heavy armor and over two hundred horses and pigs for his exploration and conquest of La Florida.

In April 1538, the de Soto expedition sailed from Spain and, two months later, arrived in Cuba. The de Soto expedition spent nearly a year in Cuba before sailing for La Florida determined to conquer the Indigenous peoples, acquire riches and establish Spanish settlements. The crew consisted of men of various skills and backgrounds, including craftsmen, engineers, farmers, merchants, priests and soldiers.

THE DE SOTO EXPEDITION LANDS IN LA FLORIDA IN 1539

In May 1539, the de Soto expedition landed in La Florida near present-day Tampa Bay (the actual site has been identified as either Charlotte Harbor or San Carlos Bay). De Soto named the land Espíritu Santo after the Holy Spirit. He had no map of the interior of La Florida, only an idea of the route he would take and a hint from the Narváez expedition regarding the type of Indigenous people he would encounter along his journey.

The de Soto landing party heard from the Uzita chiefdom that a Christian man was living in a nearby settlement. They eventually located Juan Ortiz, who was living with the indigenous Mocoso people. Ortiz was a Spaniard who was captured by the Uzita people eleven years earlier while looking for the Narváez expedition and had been stranded in La Florida ever since that time. Since Ortiz had learned the indigenous Timucua language, he became the de Soto expedition's interpreter.

As the de Soto expedition traveled northward through La Florida, Ortiz was able to communicate with various Timucua-speaking tribes. He also recruited guides from tribes that spoke different dialects or languages which enabled the Spanish to communication with various other Indigenous peoples.

The expedition engaged in armed conflicts and were ambushed by various tribes of Indigenous people throughout their journey through La Florida. De Soto decided to build a winter encampment at Anhaica, the capital of the Apalachee people, near present-day Tallahassee. The Apalachee people occasionally attacked and raided de Soto's camp for the duration of the time the expedition was in their territory.

De Soto sent a detachment of men north into present-day Georgia to scout for travel routes and large Native settlements that could be potentially

The De Soto Monument is located four miles west of Bradenton and marks the location where the de Soto expedition landed in Florida on May 30, 1539. Postcard circa 1940s. *Author's collection.*

raided for food, shelter and riches. The two smaller, highly maneuverable caravel ships in his fleet were sent westward into the Gulf of Mexico to continue exploring the region. The caravels reached present-day Pensacola Bay and then returned to the expedition's rendezvous point in February 1540.

Archaeological evidence of de Soto's first winter encampment was discovered in 1987 on land that includes the home of the former governor of Florida, John W. Martin, near the Apalachee Parkway in Tallahassee. The physical evidence uncovered includes copper coins, glass trade beads, Spanish olive jar shards, links of chain mail armor, an iron tip of a crossbow bolt and the jawbone of a pig, which are not native to North America and were brought ashore by de Soto's expedition as a source of food. This land is now the five-acre DeSoto Site Historic State Park.

THE NORTHEASTERN JOURNEY

In March 1540, de Soto abandoned the expedition's winter encampment and traveled into present-day Georgia. The expedition was in search of the Cofitachequi kingdom, which they had been informed was one of the largest and wealthiest in the region. They encountered several smaller tribes of Indigenous people, including the Ichisi, Toa, Altamaha and Cofaqui, who assisted them with food, travel and information. Fearing the approaching de Soto expedition, the Capachequi tribe abandoned their village and fled into the swamps. De Soto looted their village of all available food supplies and continued his journey in search of the Cofitachequi kingdom.

The expedition stayed in Coosa territory for over a month and then kidnapped their chief and his sister and held them as hostages. Other Coosa people were enslaved as laborers for the expedition.

When the expedition located the Cofitachequi kingdom, they found it decimated by a smallpox pandemic. There were no riches and only a meager supply of fresh food that could be looted.

On October 18, 1540, the Mobilian tribe attacked the de Soto expedition in what is known as the Battle of Mabila. Using horses and advanced weaponry, the de Soto expedition burned the village of Mabila to the ground and managed to win the grueling nine-hour battle. However, de Soto suffered his greatest losses of the journey: over 200 men were killed and 150 wounded. The Mobilian people suffered an estimated 2,500 to 3,000 deaths. The Battle of Mabila is one of the bloodiest skirmishes in recorded North American history. Considering the historical significance of Mabila, its exact location is one of American archaeology's greatest mysteries.

Around May 21, 1541, de Soto reached the eastern banks of the Mississippi River. After a month of planning and building flatboats, he and his men crossed the river at night to avoid hostile Indigenous people. De Soto's crew became the first known Europeans and Africans to cross the great river.

Indigenous guides informed de Soto that wilderness and no large kingdoms or settlements were located to the north and west of his encampment in present-day Arkansas.

THE DEATH OF HERNANDO DE SOTO

On May 21, 1542, de Soto died of fever in the kingdom of Guachoya (most likely near present-day McArthur, Arkansas, or in Louisiana). His death and burial were concealed from local Indigenous people because he caused mistrust and dissent by claiming himself a deity. The actual site of his burial remains unknown.

THE ENDING OF THE DE SOTO EXPLORATION

By the time of de Soto's death, the expedition had lost nearly half of its people and many of the survivors were sick or injured. The new leaders decided that after three years of unsuccessful searching in La Florida for riches, sites for Spanish colonization and passages to the Pacific, it was time to end the de Soto expedition and find their way to Mexico City.

Of the more than 600 people who began the de Soto expedition, about 311 survived to reach Mexico City.

The most lasting effect of the de Soto expedition was its changing of the Spanish Crown's attitude about the worthiness of its territories north of Mexico, which resulted in later expeditions and the European development of La Florida.

CHAPTER 4

INDIGENOUS PEOPLES DECIMATED

In 1513, when the Spanish conquistador Juan Ponce de León landed his expedition in La Florida, the Indigenous peoples were organized into around 200 tribes with a total population of around 350,000 throughout the peninsular area. Ancestors of Florida's Indigenous peoples had lived in the region for more than 14,000 years. Only 250 years after Ponce de León set foot in Florida, almost all its Indigenous peoples and tribes had disappeared from existence. Some tribes actually ceased to exist within just a few decades after European contact.

How could such a widespread demographic catastrophe occur in Florida in such a short period of time?

THE BEGINNING OF THE END

Ponce de León paved the way for permanent European colonization in mainland North America. However, it also marked the beginning of the end for most of Florida's Indigenous peoples. Archaeological evidence and colonial documentation suggest that almost immediately following contact with Europeans, the Indigenous people of Florida were exposed to infectious diseases such as chicken pox, influenza, measles, plague, scarlet fever, smallpox, tuberculosis and typhoid. All these European-introduced diseases were deadly to Florida's Indigenous peoples, who had no immunity against them.

A depiction of Saturiwa, a Timucuan chief in northeast Florida. In 1564, the French and, later, the Spaniards, in 1565, established settlements within or near his chiefdom. *Courtesy of Museum of Florida History. Photograph by author.*

STRESSES OF EARLY EUROPEAN COLONIZATION IN FLORIDA

In addition to the pandemics that killed tens of thousands of Florida's Indigenous peoples, European contact resulted in enslavement, warfare, annihilation of their cultures and religions and the eventual depopulation, collapse and disappearance of almost all their tribes.

Although Spain initially claimed Florida in 1513, its European foe France began building Fort Caroline (near present-day Jacksonville) in July 1564. During France's brief occupation of Fort Caroline, the French settlers interacted with local Indigenous peoples, mainly the Timucuans, engaged in trade and skirmishes and most likely spread European-introduced diseases.

Pedro Menéndez de Avilés, commander of Spain's Caribbean fleet, founded St. Augustine in 1565 and destroyed Fort Caroline in the same year. De Avilés then banished the French survivors from Florida. This brief French encounter in Florida most likely had an adverse effect on the Native population of the area.

The Spanish government in St. Augustine and its colonists quickly moved to control and manipulate Florida's Indigenous peoples and exploit their food sources and lands. The Spanish intimidated the Indigenous people by making it clear that they possessed superior military weaponry.

De Avilés's Spanish contract for colonization stated he was to convert the native people to Christianity. He arranged for Catholic priests and Jesuits to begin missionizing Florida's Indigenous peoples.

SPANISH MISSIONS IN FLORIDA

Ten Jesuit missions attached to presidios were established in Florida soon after the founding of St. Augustine. These presidios were built at major harbors with the goal of preventing other European powers from establishing colonies on land claimed by the Spanish Crown. However, several problems, including lack of supplies, hurricane damage and skirmishes with Indigenous peoples, led to the abandonment of most presidios by the early 1570s.

In 1572, due to failure to convert significant numbers of Indigenous people to Christianity, disagreements with Spanish soldiers and the murder of several missionaries by Indigenous people, the Jesuits abandoned their missions and sailed away from Florida.

In 1573, Franciscan friars came to Florida and began setting up missions in the St. Augustine area. At this time, St. Augustine was the only Spanish settlement in Florida that had a reliable flow of supplies and adequate military protection to operate missions. The missions served the Spanish in several ways. Converting Indigenous peoples to Christianity made them Spanish subjects instead of potential military foes, and the Indigenous people provided a relatively inexpensive labor force, which supplied food and services for the entire colony.

By 1587, Spanish colonization had expanded northward along the Atlantic coast, and the Franciscan friars had established new missions.

In 1606, the Spanish missions started to expand westward into the Apalachee Territory, near present-day Tallahassee. Transportation between the missions and Spanish settlements was limited to waterways and animal and footpath trails. Missions were spaced about one day's walk from one another.

In the 1680s, a traversable road called El Camino Real (the Royal Road) was used to connect the settlements and over one hundred missions throughout northern Florida. During the Spanish mission era, El Camino Real provided sufficient transportation to allow people, food and other goods to flow within the colony's widespread missions and settlements and many Indigenous villages.

The network of Spanish missions operated successfully for over one hundred years as Indigenous people traded food and labor for European tools, shelter and protection. However, conversion to Christianity eroded traditional Indigenous religions, cultures and lifestyles, and their populations continued to be decimated by outbreaks of European-introduced diseases.

In 1701, the English, French and Spanish European powers engaged in a conflict over control of the North American continent: Queen Anne's War (1702–13). This conflict led to disastrous consequences for Florida's Spanish missions and Indigenous peoples as it contributed to the destruction of the mission network in Florida.

ENGLISH SLAVE RAIDING INTO FLORIDA

Starting in 1680, the English Carolinian army and its Yamasee and Apalachicola Indian allies attacked various Spanish missions, starting along the present-day Georgia coast, causing their abandonment. Most Spanish missions were poorly defended, resulting in their buildings being burned, food and supplies looted, priests and European settlers uprooted and some Indigenous people killed. Many of the Indigenous survivors were captured and taken to Charleston to be sold into slavery.

In 1702, a large force of English soldiers and their allies landed on Amelia Island with intentions to destroy St. Augustine. These forces defeated a small Spanish garrison on Amelia Island that was stationed at a fortified tower. The army proceeded to march southward, attacking and destroying all the missions between Amelia Island and St. Augustine.

The town of St. Augustine was then besieged, and most of it was burned to the ground. The Spanish garrison at the fortification of Castillo de San Marcos managed to hold its ground and withstand the siege.

In December 1702, the English army and its allies retreated from St. Augustine; however, they captured five hundred Indigenous people and took them to the slave markets in Charleston.

THE APALACHEE MASSACRE

Between 1702 and 1709, a series of English attacks into northern Florida organized by Carolina Governor James Moore managed to destroy most of the Apalachee Spanish missions and Indigenous villages in the region. These attacks are now known as the Apalachee Massacre.

The most devastating Spanish mission raids occurred in early and mid-1704, when English Carolinian forces assisted by their Indian allies essentially destroyed the Apalachee mission system. Hundreds of Indigenous men and thousands of women and children were enslaved and taken to Carolinian plantations or sold to plantation owners in the West Indies.

COLLAPSE OF THE SPANISH MISSIONS IN FLORIDA

As a result of the raids and destruction of the Spanish missions, ten to twelve thousand Indigenous people were enslaved and removed from Florida by English forces and their Indian allies. Most of the farming and ranching operations in Florida were destroyed or left with no labor force, which had devastating effects on the entire economy of the colony.

Most of the Indigenous people who had successfully adapted to colonial life within the Spanish mission system were scattered, enslaved or killed. Survivors had no sustainable Native villages to return to, as most were either abandoned or destroyed.

MORE ATTACKS FROM THE NORTH

With the Spanish missions in northern Florida destroyed and little Spanish military presence outside of the St. Augustine area, Indian tribes such as the Lower Creeks, the Savannahs and the Yamasee raided Florida all the way south into the Florida Keys. These Indian raiders were armed with rifles, powder and shot they obtained from trading deerskins and furs with English settlers in the Virginia and Carolina colonies. Many of Florida's remaining Indigenous settlements were defenseless against such firepower and were looted and burned and their peoples killed or enslaved by these Indian raiders from the north.

INDIANS FROM THE NORTH FLEE TO FLORIDA

Beginning in 1715, several Native Indian groups, including the Yamasee, Creeks and Apalachicola, rebelled against English colonists, and many fled to St. Augustine, where they were welcomed by the Spanish government and Franciscan priests. Other groups of Native Indian refugees from the north started to resettle villages that were previously abandoned by Florida's Indigenous peoples. Spanish officials in St. Augustine attempted to recruit additional Native Indians from the north to reestablish agricultural production in the colony, but those efforts were mostly unsuccessful.

New mission towns were established around St. Augustine and in the Apalachee Territory. A new wave of Native Indians from north of Florida raided these mission towns and enslaved many of their inhabitants. In a twist of fate, some of the Yamasee people, who had previously been raiders and slavers and later fled to Florida, were captured and enslaved by Creek Indians who were resettling villages in northern Florida.

EUROPEAN-INTRODUCED DISEASES, WARFARE AND SLAVERY

By the early 1760s, most of Florida's Indigenous peoples who were settled in the peninsular area at the time of European contact in 1513 no longer existed. European influence rapidly caused Indigenous cultures to change and evolve as their people voluntarily and involuntarily migrated in and out of Florida. Indigenous people also merged with other groups within and outside of Florida in order to survive and adjust to their rapidly changing world.

When the Spanish turned Florida over to the English in 1763, only a small number of Indigenous people still identified with their original tribes. As the Spanish population in Florida withdrew to Cuba, many of these remaining Indigenous people relocated with them, while others assimilated into other tribes, such as the Yamasee and the Creeks.

In the 1760s, one small group of Apalachee people fled from Florida to Louisiana. By 1825, there were only forty-five of them alive. Today, some Apalachee descendants known as the Talimali Band of Apalachee live in Rapides Parish, Louisiana, and others in the Kisatchie National Forest near Chopin, Louisiana.

By the end of the eighteenth century, a combination of exposure to European-introduced diseases, warfare and slavery had caused the decimation of most of the original Indigenous tribes and peoples of Florida. However, some managed to assimilate into other groups that survived Indian wars with colonial powers and the United States, skirmishes with European settlers and the Indian Removal Act of 1830, which led to the horrific forced relocation of Indians in the eastern United States to lands west of the Mississippi River known as the Trail of Tears.

A physical remnant of the Indigenous Timucua people of Florida is this shell midden (circa AD 1000 to 1500), which is mostly intact but now overgrown with trees and other vegetation. It is located at Shell Bluff Park in Andalusia. *Photograph by author.*

The original Indigenous Florida peoples of the sixteenth century no longer exist on their traditional lands, but some of their descendants live today and maintain some of their original traditions, religions and political ideologies. However, these new societies in which descendants of Florida's original Indigenous peoples live are significantly different from those that existed prior to European contact and colonization.

TODAY'S NATIVE AMERICANS IN FLORIDA

Currently, there are two federally recognized Native American tribes living in Florida: the Miccosukee and the Seminoles (neither is indigenous to the state).

The Miccosukee originated from the Lower Chiaha chiefdom, which was one of the tribes of the Creek Confederacy in present-day Georgia. They migrated into Florida in the early eighteenth century as European expansion encroached into their territory. After they settled in Florida, they became part of the Seminole Nation. In 1962, they received federal recognition as an independent tribe.

The Seminoles were created from various tribes, mainly the Creeks, who migrated into Florida from present-day Georgia and Alabama during the eighteenth century as European expansion into their territories threatened their existence. The Seminoles are descendants of many Indigenous southeastern Indians, including various Indigenous Florida tribes.

Today, many Seminoles live in Oklahoma as well as Florida. The name Seminole derives from the Spanish word *cimarrón*, which means "runaway" or "wild one."

CHAPTER 5

PENSACOLA FOUNDED

The Spanish were aware of the Pensacola Bay as a natural harbor and had explored the area prior to deciding to establish a permanent settlement in the region.

In 1516, the Spanish explorer Diego de Miruelo was the first European to sail into the Pensacola Bay. Subsequent Spanish expeditions led by Pánfilo de Narváez, in 1528, and Hernando de Soto, in 1539, landed in Florida at Pensacola Bay. De Soto's expedition named the area the Bay of Ochuse after a local Indigenous tribe they encountered.

In 1559, the Spanish conquistador Tristán de Luna y Arellano established a short-lived settlement near the Pensacola Bay (which he named Bahía Santa María de Filipina). This was the first multiyear European settlement in the present-day continental United States. Just two years later, in 1561, the settlement was nearly destroyed by a massive hurricane. In the wake of the disastrous hurricane, the settlement was promptly abandoned as the northern Gulf of Mexico area of the Spanish Florida territory was deemed too dangerous to colonize; it would not be resettled until 1698.

In 1698, the Spanish established modern Pensacola due to its strategic location as a defense against French settlements in Louisiana.

The name Pensacola was most likely derived from the local Indigenous Muskogee-speaking tribe that the Spanish named Penzacola. In 1757, a royal order issued by Spanish King Ferdinand VI proclaimed the bay's name Penzacola. The spelling was later changed to Pensacola because it was easier for the Spanish to pronounce.

THE ORIGINAL ESTABLISHMENT OF PENSACOLA IN 1559

Luís de Velasco, the second viceroy of New Spain, appointed Tristán de Luna y Arellano to lead the establishment of Spanish colonies on the Gulf Coast, on the lower Atlantic Coast and in the interior of southeastern North America.

There were several goals for the establishment of these colonies. One was to enable the Franciscan friar Andrés de Olmos to establish a network of missions along the coast of the Gulf of Mexico so Indigenous people could be converted to Christianity. A second was to provide assistance and a place of refuge for shipwrecked Spaniards. A third was to peacefully establish a full trading partnership with Indigenous tribes. A fourth was to seek riches, including precious gems, silver, gold and mercury. Another was to establish a military presence to prevent the French and other European powers from claiming and colonizing lands in Florida that the Spanish asserted belonged to them because they were the first to explore the area.

On August 14, 1559, after a two-month journey through some perilous weather conditions, de Luna's fleet of 13 ships, approximately 1,550 people (1,050 colonists, servants and Mexican Indians and 500 soldiers) and 140 horses anchored in the Bay of Ochuse (Pensacola Bay).

De Luna identified a high point of land where the pueblo settlement of Santa María de Ochuse was to be built. Spanish laws and traditions provided a grid for the street layout and a building plan for the settlement, which included a governor's residence fronting a central plaza, a church, a monastery, one hundred residential lots for families and soldiers and forty lots for church and governmental use. Eighty to one hundred people from de Luna's expedition were to stay, building and organizing the pueblo settlement of Santa María de Ochuse.

De Luna discovered very few Indigenous people living around Pensacola Bay and realized that obtaining food and supplies for his large landing party was going to be a major task. Complicating the situation, just five days after the expedition landed at Pensacola Bay, a severe hurricane struck the area. The storm sank or ran ashore nine ships from the fleet, destroyed about half of the supplies and food and killed an unreported number of seamen and colonists. As starvation became a possibility, de Luna realized most of his people would need to be moved to Indigenous settlements inland where food could be obtained.

De Luna organized two scouting parties to venture into the interior of Florida and search for a place to settle, one with sustainable food sources.

A watercolor depicting Tristán de Luna y Arellano's historic landing at Pensacola Bay in August 1559, by Herbert Rudeen. *Courtesy of Pensacola Historical Society.*

The scouts found only one place with an immediate food source: an Indian village called Nanipacana (near present-day Monroe County, Alabama) that was abandoned by its people as they fled to avoid de Luna's scouts. At Nanipacana, in addition to food and fresh water sources, there were some established shelters, so de Luna decided to relocate most of his expedition to this village. In February 1560, de Luna arrived with the bulk of his expedition and renamed the village Nanipacana de Santa Cruz.

About fifty soldiers and some Black servants were left behind at Pensacola Bay to continue the task of establishing a permanent settlement and guard Spanish supplies.

By early spring of 1560, the food supplies at Nanipacana de Santa Cruz were running critically short. A large military unit accompanied by two priests was sent to find the Coosa chiefdom, which Hernando de Soto and his expedition visited in 1540. In the meantime, food shortages coupled with disciplinary problems at Nanipacana de Santa Cruz forced the now ill and weak de Luna to abandon the village and move his expedition back to the Pensacola Bay coastal area. The journey back to Santa María de Ochuse at Pensacola Bay was an arduous one. Several of the expedition's people died from drowning and starvation.

About one week after de Luna's expedition returned to Pensacola, a Spanish ship arrived with a small supply of food. Additionally, the ship carried a royal order from the viceroy of Mexico, which instructed de Luna to occupy Santa Elena (present-day South Carolina) due to the perceived threat of French colonization on Spanish territory.

On August 10, 1560, de Luna sent three ships from his fleet to Santa Elena, but they were severely damaged by tropical storms and forced to return to Mexico. The viceroy of Mexico blamed de Luna for the expedition's failure to secure Santa Elena.

During the winter of 1560, de Luna's Pensacola settlement was hampered by bad morale and mutiny, which jeopardized the work on the colony and threatened its future.

On January 30, 1561, after receiving many complaints and disappointed with the lack of progress on the Pensacola colony, the viceroy of Mexico relieved de Luna of his command and appointed Ángel de Villafañe, the Spanish conquistador and ship captain, as the new governor. It was not until the first week of April 1561 that Villafañe arrived and informed de Luna of his dismissal. De Luna accepted his dismissal gracefully and left Pensacola, returning to Spain to address the king regarding his failure to establish a permanent settlement in Florida.

Villafañe was tasked with evacuating most of the expedition from Pensacola to Havana and arranging a new contingent of soldiers to occupy Santa Elena. A group of about sixty settlers and soldiers under Captain Diego de Biedma remained in Pensacola to guard the area and maintain a Spanish presence in their Florida territory.

While Villafañe was in Cuba, many of the expedition deserted him, and he was forced to sail to Santa Elena with three ships and only seventy-five crewmen. Villafañe managed to occupy Santa Elena with his small militia force.

On June 14, 1561, Villafañe's small fleet was decimated by a strong storm, which forced him to abandon Santa Elena and return to New Spain. It was reported that he stopped in Pensacola Bay and evacuated all the settlers and soldiers he had left behind.

There is no historical record of anyone from the de Luna expedition remaining in Pensacola by July 1561. In every practical or functional sense, de Luna's expedition to establish a permanent settlement in Florida had failed.

The Spanish Crown was furious about the squandered expenditures, the loss of life and the failure of de Luna's expedition to establish a permanent settlement in Florida. As a consequence, the northern Gulf of Mexico area of the Spanish Florida territory was left undefended against colonization and conquest by rival European powers for the following 137 years.

"MODERN" PENSACOLA ESTABLISHED IN 1698

On June 13, 1694, the Spanish Crown authorized the establishment of a settlement at Pensacola Bay in an effort to prevent other European powers, mainly France and England, from establishing colonies along the north and east coasts of the Gulf of Mexico. However, due to Spain's engagement in King William's War (1689–97), the settlement at Pensacola Bay was delayed until after the war ended.

In November 1698, the Spanish began building a new settlement on Santa Rosa Island at Pensacola Bay under the leadership of the Spanish governor Andrés de Arriola y Guzmán. The Presidio Santa Maria de Galve, a village, a church and Fort San Carlos de Austria were the first major building projects erected. This marked the beginning of a permanent Spanish settlement in and military occupation of the Pensacola Bay area, the first since the failed de Luna expedition nearly a century and a half earlier.

In May 1719, the French overtook Fort San Carlos de Austria and assumed control of Pensacola. The viceroy of Mexico organized a fleet of fifteen ships and 1,200 troops under the command of Alfonso Carrascosa de la Torre to retake Pensacola from the French. On August 14, 1719, Carrascosa arrived in Pensacola Bay, fired on the French ships and surrounded Fort San Carlos de Austria. French forces soon forced Carrascosa and his Spanish troops to retreat from Pensacola.

In 1722, a hurricane drove the French out of Pensacola; however, they burned and destroyed the fort and most of the buildings in the settlement before they abandoned it. The Spanish reclaimed Pensacola in 1722 and built a second settlement on Santa Rosa Island. A new presidio was built and named Presidio Isla de Santa Rosa (near the site of present-day Fort Pickens).

In 1754, a disastrous hurricane destroyed most of the settlement on Santa Rosa Island, forcing the Spanish to relocate to the mainland. A third Spanish settlement, called Presidio San Miguel de Pensacola, was built near present-day downtown Pensacola.

In 1763, following Spain's defeat in the Seven Years' War (also known as the French and Indian War), Florida, including Pensacola, was handed over to the British. Florida was divided into two parts: West Florida and East Florida. Pensacola became the capital of West Florida.

On May 8, 1779, Spain officially entered the American Revolutionary War allied with the United States against the British. In February 1781, Bernardo de Gálvez, the governor of Spanish Louisiana, launched aggressions, known as the Siege of Pensacola, against British military positions in Pensacola.

Fort San Carlos de Barrancas is located in Pensacola and was built in 1787 by the Spanish. *Postcard circa 1970s. Author's collection.*

Spanish and French naval vessels blockaded Pensacola Bay and attacked Pensacola with cannon fire. The British surrendered on May 8, 1781. The Spanish officially reclaimed control of Pensacola on May 10, 1781.

Following the American Revolutionary War, the Spanish held control of Pensacola, and all of Florida, until the Adams-Onís Treaty ceded the territory to the United States in 1821.

CHAPTER 6

ST. AUGUSTINE FOUNDED

On June 22, 1564, René Goulaine de Laudonnière established a French colonial settlement on the banks of the St. Johns River near present-day Jacksonville that became known as Fort Caroline. French King Charles IX was attempting to establish a foothold in present-day Florida and South Carolina to add to New France (territory colonized by France in North America starting in 1534). New France formally ended with the cession of its territories to Great Britain and Spain in 1763.

On March 20, 1565, King Philip II of Spain issued a three-year contract to the Spanish admiral Pedro Menéndez de Avilés. This contract granted Menéndez the title of adelantado (Spanish governor) of Florida and authorized him to explore and establish a permanent colony in Florida, which would also protect the Spanish treasure fleet. Menéndez was also commissioned to expel all non-Spanish colonists and militia forces from Spanish territory in North America between Terranova (Newfoundland) and St. Joseph's Bay on the Gulf of Mexico.

On August 28, 1565, the feast day of St. Augustine of Hippo, Avilés's fleet of five ships carrying six hundred soldiers and colonists, including twenty-six women and their children, sighted a harbor along the Florida coastline. Menéndez named the harbor San Agustín (St. Augustine) in honor of the patron saint of his hometown of Avilés, Spain.

The five Spanish ships sailed north in search of the French settlement of Fort Caroline. At the mouth of the River May (St. Johns River), a French fleet of ships commanded by Jean Ribault was anchored after unloading settlers, supplies, reinforcement soldiers and weapons to defend Fort Caroline against Spanish intrusion. The French ships slipped their anchors and outmaneuvered and sailed away from the weighted-down Spanish ships. Menéndez then sailed his ships southward to the harbor of St. Augustine in search of a site to establish a Spanish settlement.

On September 8, 1565, Menéndez anchored his nine-hundred-ton flagship, *San Pelayo*, in the harbor of St. Augustine as it was too large to navigate into the shallow inlet. The four smaller ships sailed into the inlet, where Menéndez and his soldiers and colonists came ashore near the Indigenous Timucua village of Seloy.

Menéndez immediately began making plans to establish a permanent Spanish settlement, which was also named St. Augustine, in and around the village of Seloy. Menéndez was also strategizing military plans to expel the French from Fort Caroline, which he suspected was only a short distance to the north of St. Augustine. This French settlement presented an immediate threat to Spain's claim to the Florida territory.

THE ESTABLISHMENT OF ST. AUGUSTINE IN 1565

Menéndez ordered his men to fortify the council house of Seloy by digging trenches around its perimeter and reinforcing its walls with earthworks. The council house became Menéndez's makeshift fort and warehouse for the fleet's supplies.

A christening ceremony accompanied by Chaplain Francisco López de Mendoza Grajales, trumpets, gunfire and a notary officially handed possession of Florida to Menéndez. This was the beginning of the Spanish municipality of St. Augustine.

Supplies were offloaded from the flagship *San Pelayo*, and Menéndez ordered the ship and its crew southward to Hispaniola to bring reinforcements back to St. Augustine.

Meanwhile, Ribault and his French fleet were in pursuit of the *San Pelayo* as a hurricane was fast approaching.

THE DESTRUCTION OF FRENCH FORT CAROLINE

As the French fleet was occupied pursuing the *San Pelayo*, Menéndez organized five hundred soldiers and marched overland from St. Augustine

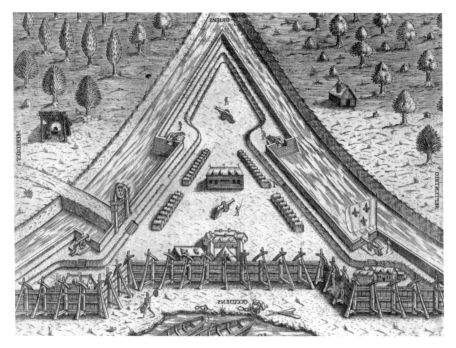

Sixteenth-century etching of Fort Caroline. *Courtesy of Wikimedia Commons.*

to locate and destroy Fort Caroline. Menéndez and his Spanish forces broke through Fort Caroline's main gate on September 20, 1565, and attacked the French soldiers and colonists. The Spanish captured and executed about one hundred men but spared the lives of about fifty women and children. About forty-five Frenchmen, including Jacques Le Moyne de Morgues, René Laudonnière and Nicolas Le Challeux, managed to escape on the remaining ships, planning to sail back to France. The following day, Indigenous people captured some of the French escapees and turned them over to Menéndez at Fort Caroline (which he renamed to Fort San Mateo).

Menéndez ordered most of his Spanish forces to remain at Fort San Mateo to guard the captured supplies and fortifications, while he and a smaller group of Spanish soldiers marched back to St. Augustine to continue fortifying the new municipality in preparation for a suspected French attack.

About a week later, Indigenous people informed Menéndez that a hurricane had wrecked two of Ribault's French ships south of St. Augustine (near present-day Ponce de Leon Inlet) and about 140 survivors were marching north along the beach in an attempt to reach Fort Caroline. Menéndez quickly organized a group of Spanish soldiers and issued orders to march south to intercept and capture the French shipwreck survivors.

THE MATANZAS MASSACRE OF THE FRENCH

A group of about forty Spaniards spotted the shipwrecked French at Matanzas Inlet. Dressed in French attire, Menéndez approached the French and notified them that the Spaniards had defeated Fort Caroline. Menéndez demanded the French surrender, which they did. After all their

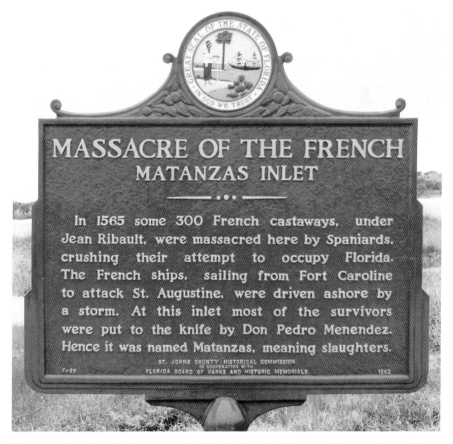

Massacre of the French, Matanzas Inlet. Florida Board of Parks and Historic Memorials. *Photograph by author.*

arms and ammunition had been handed over to the Spaniards, the French prisoners crossed the lagoon in groups of ten with their hands bound behind them. The French did not know the Spaniards had a large force of soldiers hiding in ambush.

Ten Catholics were discovered within the ranks of the 140 French prisoners. These Catholics were placed in a boat and sailed to St. Augustine. The remainder of the prisoners confessed themselves to be Protestants and were marched a short distance to the north. Soon afterward, Menéndez ordered the defenseless French executed, massacre-style, and beheaded.

Indigenous people then informed Menéndez that Ribault was marching north toward Fort Caroline with an additional two hundred men. Menéndez and his troops laid in wait at Matanzas Inlet until Ribault's entire French party arrived.

After reaching Matanzas Inlet, Ribault realized he was outnumbered and waved a white flag of surrender. Menéndez informed Ribault that his forces had captured Fort Caroline (which soon after was destroyed by an accidental fire) and that many Frenchmen were killed during the conflict. Ribault then saw the bodies of some of the Frenchmen who had been massacred at Matanzas Inlet twelve days earlier and offered Menéndez a considerable amount of money (one hundred thousand ducats) to allow his party to go free. Ribault also asked Menéndez for a ship so he and his party could leave Florida and sail back to France. Menéndez refused and ordered all the French prisoners to be bound with their hands tied behind them. Seventeen Catholics were identified in this party, and they were set free.

Menéndez ordered the remainder of Ribault's French party, all non-Catholics, executed in the same manner as the previous massacre of the French. Ribault was saved for last; however, he, too, was executed and beheaded. A total of around three hundred men were brutally executed by order of Menéndez. The defeat of Fort Caroline and the following bloody massacres at Matanzas Inlet ended French attempts to colonize Florida.

ST. AUGUSTINE'S ENDURANCE

St. Augustine, founded in 1565, became the first permanent European settlement in La Florida. The city was the most significant settlement in the region for nearly three hundred years. Today, St. Augustine is the oldest continuously inhabited European-established settlement in the continental United States.

CHAPTER 7

RANCHING AND CATTLE HERITAGE

In the sixteenth century, Spanish explorers and settlers introduced cattle and horses into Florida. This makes Florida the first area in the present-day United States to have had cattle and horses. Organized ranching in Florida began in 1565 as a necessity, to provide beef to military personnel and colonists after the founding of St. Augustine. During the 1600s, many Native Americans learned agricultural and cattle-tending skills from Spanish clergymen while living and working at Spanish Catholic missions in Florida.

Significant cattle ranches were established in Spanish Florida from 1655 to 1700 as a means to provide food and leather for Spanish military garrisons and early settlers. By 1700, there were extensive ranches located along the St. Johns River (near present-day Palatka), in Apalache (present-day Tallahassee) and in the present-day Gainesville area, as well as some smaller ranches north of St. Augustine that stretched into southern Georgia.

British and Creek Indian raids into Spanish Florida in 1702 and 1704 plundered and destroyed many ranches. For the remainder of the 1700s, Native Americans owned and managed large herds of cattle. Some of their cattle were rounded up while running wild, and others were purchased from the Spanish. Interestingly, Ahaya (1710–1783), who was the first chief of the Alachua band of the Seminole Indian tribe, was known to European Americans as Cowkeeper because he owned a large herd of cattle.

During Florida's British period (1763–83), ranchers from Georgia and the Carolinas moved into Spanish Florida and, along with English planters and Creek Indians, built up substantial cattle herds.

"FLORIDA CRACKER" OR "CRACKER COWBOYS"

Florida Cracker and *Cracker Cowboys* are historical terms that refer to the cattlemen of Florida from the late eighteenth through the twentieth century. Florida Crackers were different from traditional American cowboys as they did not use lassos (a rope with a noose at one end) to control and corral herds of cattle; instead, they used dogs and braided buckskin whips (called Florida Cracker Whips). Florida Crackers were important in Florida history as they developed a unique culture and helped stimulate the state's economy and growth.

By the second half of the eighteenth century, the growing cattle populations and their economic value gave rise to rustling. European Americans and Indians both engaged in rustling and stole cattle from one another as well.

In addition to the dangers of rustlers, harsh conditions in Florida challenged cattlemen, as they had to guard against attacks from wild animals including bears, panthers and wolves. Some cattle drives lasted weeks or months through Florida's rough terrain. Conditions such as dense scrub woodlands, marshes, burning heat and humidity, muddied trails and destructive winds and flooding from occasional tropical storms and hurricanes hampered cattle drives.

The cattle population in Florida dramatically increased from the 1840s to the American Civil War as Florida became second in the South to Texas in per capita value of livestock. The Florida Armed Occupation Act of 1842 was passed as an incentive to increase the population of Florida by offering two hundred thousand acres of land to White settlers. Some of this land was the former property of the Seminole Indians forced to move to Indian reservations in Oklahoma. This act enticed many cattlemen from Georgia, Alabama and the Carolinas to relocate cattle herds as they homesteaded in Florida. Some of the newly introduced cattle interbred with the semi-feral Florida Cracker cows.

Any head of a family could claim 160 acres under the Florida Armed Occupation Act of 1842. The act's stipulated conditions were: the claimant must be a White male resident of Florida (not owning 160 acres of land before applying to the Land Office); he or his heirs must reside on the property for five consecutive years, build a house and clear and cultivate five acres of land on the property during the first year; and the property had to be two or more miles away from a garrisoned military post.

By the 1850s, ranchers were grazing and running cattle on huge open ranges in central and south Florida as the cattle trade accounted for a sizable part of the state's economy.

The 1860 census recorded 388,060 head of cattle in Florida. At this time, Florida was oftentimes referred to as the "last great frontier east of the Mississippi River."

Several nineteenth century wars—the Second Seminole War (1835–42), the Third Seminole War (1855–58), the American Civil War (1861–65) and the Spanish American War (April 21 to December 10, 1898)—provided economic opportunities for Florida cattlemen as they supplied U.S. military forces with leather, meat and tallow.

FLORIDA'S CONFEDERATE "COW CAVALRY"

During the American Civil War, the Confederate States of America created a "cow cavalry" to protect cattle herds from Union raids.

After the fall of the Confederate stronghold of Vicksburg, Mississippi, in July 1863, Florida was divided into five commissary districts. The Confederacy requested three thousand head of cattle per week be shipped north to supply foodstuffs for the Army of Northern Virginia, the Army of Tennessee and several garrisons.

Many factors hampered cattle being driven north to supply the major war fronts, including dwindling pastureland and fodder along the supply routes, Confederate deserters turned rustlers, rising discontent with the war effort and cattlemen's reluctance to accept Confederate promissory notes as their value was suspect.

Nine companies of Confederate cavalry were organized, consisting mostly of men too old or too young to fight in the war, to protect the supply line of cattle, and they became known as the Cow Cavalry. The main job of the Cow Cavalry was to assist and protect the cattle drives as they moved north out of Florida. They had some success, which caught the attention of Union forces, as they managed to deliver cattle to several Confederate garrisons. The Cow Cavalry actually helped the Confederacy prolong the American Civil War.

The Union attempted to cut off the cattle supply from Florida, and this effort resulted in the Battle of Olustee on February 20, 1864, which was the largest battle fought in Florida during the American Civil War.

FLORIDA CRACKER COWS

The Florida Cracker cow (sometimes referred to as Florida Scrub) is an American breed of cattle. These cattle were first introduced into Spanish Florida from Cuba in 1565. They were bred for meat and milk and to perform work such as providing power or leverage to move loads. Florida Cracker cows were the principal cattle breed in Florida until the early twentieth century. Many lived in semi-feral conditions, surviving on native forage; were tolerant of high heat; and became immune to many diseases. Indiscriminate crossbreeding and the introduction of heat-tolerant and domesticated cattle breeds led to the near extinction of the breed by the middle of the twentieth century. Since the 1970s, the Florida state government has created conservation programs to save the breed. In 1989, the Florida Cracker Cattle Association was established with the stated mission to "preserve these cattle that were so important to the agricultural history of Florida and that provided the foundation for today's cattle industry." In 2018, the Florida Cracker cow was declared the official Florida state heritage cattle breed. Recently, the breeding programs have had moderate success: the population of Florida Cracker cows is estimated to be as high as five thousand.

In May 1865, the war was coming to an end. Union forces occupied Tampa and demanded that all Confederate holdouts surrender. On June 5, 1865, the Cow Cavalry surrendered to the Union.

After the American Civil War ended, markets in the United States, Cuba and the Bahamas expanded the cattle trade to the point that Florida became the nation's leading exporter. From 1868 to 1878, Florida cattlemen sold and exported over 1.6 million cattle to Cuba.

FLORIDA'S MODERN CATTLE INDUSTRY

The Cuban demand for Florida cattle declined early in the twentieth century, and cattlemen began shipping more cattle to domestic markets via the railroads.

Since the 1930s, cattlemen have been crossbreeding native Florida cattle with Angus, Brahman, Charolais, Hereford, Limousin and Shorthorn breeds,

Florida Cracker cows on Newberry Road outside Gainesville, circa 1930. *Courtesy of Wikimedia Commons.*

A grazing Florida Cracker Horse. *Courtesy of Wikimedia Commons.*

FLORIDA CRACKER HORSES

Ponce de León first brought horses to Florida during his second voyage in 1521. During the sixteenth century, the Spanish continued to introduce horse breeds into Florida, including Andalusians, Barbs, Garranos, Sorraias and Spanish Jennets. These Spanish-ancestry horses had low-set tails, short backs, sloping shoulders and wide foreheads. Florida Cracker cowboys used them to drive cattle, and they eventually developed into the breed known as the Florida Cracker Horse, known for agility, endurance and speed. From the mid-sixteenth century into the 1930s, the Florida Cracker Horse was common in the southeastern United States. On July 1, 2008, the Florida Cracker Horse was declared the official state horse of Florida. Due to a dwindling breed population caused by crossbreeding, urbanization and the decline of traditional ranching, the Florida Cracker Horse is now listed as an endangered breed.

which has increased size, resistance to heat and insects and hardiness and improved overall meat quality. This successful crossbreeding has led to the development of hybrid breeds, including Braford and Brangus.

Today, Florida is predominately a cow-calf state, with fifteen thousand beef producers and ranked thirteen in the nation in overall cattle numbers. Approximately half of all Florida agricultural land is involved in cattle production. The major cattle "crop" is calves, which are mainly shipped around the country to be finished and processed into beef. There are more than one million cows in Florida, which produce over eight hundred thousand calves annually. Florida also has over one hundred thousand dairy cows that produce over two billion pounds of raw milk annually.

CHAPTER 8

INTRICATE CONNECTIONS TO SLAVERY

The traditional Hollywood versions of slavery in the United States conjure up visions of antebellum plantations with Black people (historically referred to as "negroes") picking cotton or tobacco in expansive fields on scorching hot sunny days. The story of slavery in Florida is a lot broader and more complicated than the typical fictitious, and historically inaccurate, Hollywood imagery in movies such as *Gone with the Wind*. Intricate connections to slavery are woven deep into Florida's history, starting with the European invasion.

When Spain first claimed Florida in 1513 and then followed with expeditions and settlements, free and enslaved Black people accompanied the Spaniards on these epic journeys. Documents spanning Spanish Florida's history record African-born Black slaves working with both Native Indians and Europeans. Throughout the 1500s and into the 1600s, only a small number of enslaved Black people were imported into Florida as there were no large mines or plantations at that time requiring significant labor forces.

In 1693, a Spanish royal decree vowed freedom and sanctuary for enslaved Black people who escaped, mainly from the southern British colonies (Georgia, Maryland, Virginia and Carolina, which would be divided into North and South Carolina in 1712), and fled to Spanish Florida if they accepted Catholic baptism. Men, if able, were required to serve a number of years in the Spanish militia. The government of Spanish Florida found it in its best interest to welcome escaped slaves: they boosted the population, expanded the economy by adding skills and labor into the workforce and served as security forces who had the extra incentive of not being captured and sold back into slavery. Some of these escaped slaves became known as *Maroons* (descendants of Africans who formed their own settlements, typically near Native Indian towns and reservations).

Slavery in Florida under Spanish rule was not as harsh as under British or U.S. rule. The Spanish allowed slaves some rights, such as property ownership and marriage (including mixed-race marriage, where children of mixed race could inherit property), and the enslaved had the ability to purchase their freedom. If Black people were free and were Catholic, there was no legal discrimination (unfair or prejudicial distinctions based on race).

By the early eighteenth century, many Maroon communities (groups of formerly enslaved Black people and their descendants, along with people of mixed race) had organized in Florida, and they typically cooperated with the Spanish government. Throughout the eighteenth and into the early nineteenth century, English colonists increasingly threatened Spanish Florida's governmental authority by invading its territory to capture escaped slaves and steal property, such as livestock. Private slave catchers (people employed to track down and capture escaped slaves and return them to their enslavers) also raided Spanish Florida. This was a lucrative trade during this time.

By the end of the First Spanish Period in 1763, slaves accounted for 13 percent of Florida's population.

BLACK SEMINOLES

Black Seminoles (sometimes referred to as Afro-Seminoles) are an ethnic group of mixed Native American Indian and African origin who originally settled in Florida starting in the mid-1700s. They descended from Seminole Indians, freedmen (emancipated Black slaves) and escaped Black slaves. Black Seminoles lived in distinct communities near Seminole Indian settlements. Some Black Seminoles were actually enslaved by the Seminole Indians (mostly held by chiefs). The Seminole system of slavery differed from the British and Spanish systems of chattel slavery (one person having total ownership of one or more human beings). Since the Seminole Indians were mainly herders and hunters, they required Black Seminole slaves to turn over a portion of their agricultural harvests to supplement their food banks. Black Seminoles typically lived without oversight from their Seminole owners and served as advisors, field hands and interpreters. They were also armed for their security and fought as warriors with the Seminole Indians. Many were known as fierce fighters. The Seminole Indians also protected the Black Seminoles (free or enslaved) against White slavers and intruders.

BRITISH PERIOD (1763–83)

When the Seven Years' War, a global conflict known in North America as the French and Indian War, ended in 1763 with the signing of the Treaty of Paris, Great Britain was awarded Spanish Florida. The British divided the territory into two colonies: East Florida and West Florida. The vast number of Spanish citizens and others loyal to Spain that were living in Florida moved out of the colony. The British awarded large land grants to encourage settlement in the colony and to construct large-scale plantation enterprises and improve roadways to build up an industrial economy. Slave labor was used to construct, operate and manage British Florida's economic base. The British purchased most of their slaves from Africa via the transatlantic slave trade, and Black people became a large percentage of Florida's population. Many times during the British rule of Florida, Blacks outnumbered Whites.

Plantations were very difficult and expensive to establish in Florida. The enslaved labor force had the arduous tasks of clearing forests and thick brush, digging, dredging, damming and draining swamps before any fields could be cultivated. Slaves also built much of the colony's infrastructure, including bridges, homes, plantation buildings and roads. Slaves provided practically all the labor, both skilled and unskilled, required to operate plantations, including working in the fields, tending to livestock, harvesting and preparing crops for transport and sale and operating equipment to process sugarcane and distill rum.

Under the British system of chattel slavery, all slaves and their families were considered nonhuman property. Slaves could be sold or rented, including children, and families could be separated. If slave owners mistreated slaves by whipping, branding, raping or even murdering one or more, they faced no legal punishment. Some slave owners treated slaves well and even provided medical care, as slaves were an expensive investment. However, slaves were legally bound to their owner's oversight for life under British rule.

During the British period, slaves accounted for 65 percent of Florida's population (11,200 out of 17,300 people).

SECOND SPANISH PERIOD (1783–1821)

The 1783 Peace of Paris treaty ended the American Revolutionary War and awarded British Florida to Spain. This treaty also formally recognized the United States as an independent nation. Spain adopted the British governing practice of two separate territories: East and West Florida.

The Spanish system of slavery in Florida changed little from what it was during the First Spanish Period. Many escaped slaves from the United States began fleeing into Spanish Florida seeking freedom, tensions between the nations rose.

U.S. authorities led by General Andrew Jackson invaded Spanish Florida in an attempt to recapture escaped slaves, many of whom were living with the Seminole Indians. This aggression caused the First Seminole War (1817–18) to break out. U.S. forces burned Seminole towns and villages, seized Pensacola and St. Marks and perpetrated other acts of hostility. By this time, Spain was politically and militarily unable to protect its Florida territories from United States militarism. Spain ceded its Florida territories to the United States via the Adams-Onís Treaty in 1819, which went into effect in 1821.

In 1821, Florida's enslaved population numbered around four thousand, about 50 percent of the state's estimated population of 8,000.

UNITED STATES RULE (1821–61)

The United States used a system of chattel slavery and prevented escaped slaves from entering Florida as a safe haven. Many slaves were subjected to dehumanizing treatment, deprived of most civil rights and not taught to read and write, and they were subject to sale (which often broke up families).

The internal slave trade, also known as the domestic slave trade, allowed enslaved people to be transferred between slaveholders. Many slaves were purchased in the Upper South and transported to the Lower South.

In 1860, Florida's enslaved people numbered 140,424 (44 percent of the total population). By this time, all slaves in the United States were born into slavery by natural reproduction.

Committed to Jail At St. Marks, as a RUNAWAY, a Negro Man, who says his name is MILES, and that he belongs to James McNeil, of Montgomery County, Alabama. Said negro is about 5 feet 9 inches high, and about 24 years old; The owner of said Slave is requested to come forward, prove property, pay charges and take him away. ROBERT LLOYD, Jailor. July 19th, 1838. 50-tf

CENSUS OF 1855.	WHITE MALES.		WHITE FEMALES.		CHILDREN.		SLAVES.		
Marion County. NAMES:	Over 21.	Under 21.	Over 18.	Under 18.	Between 5 and 18.	In Schools.	Males.	Females.	VALUE OF.
Casters Alexander	1	1	1	2	1		2	2	3000

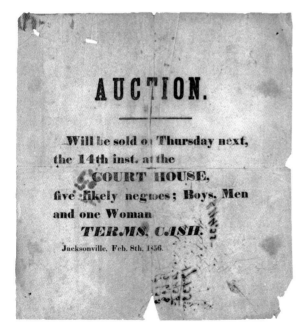

AUCTION.

Will be sold on Thursday next, the 14th inst. at the

COURT HOUSE,

five likely negroes; Boys, Men and one Woman

TERMS, CASH.

Jacksonville, Feb. 8th, 1856.

Top: A newspaper advertisement announcing the capture of a runaway enslaved "Negro Man" named Miles in St. Marks, Florida. *From the* Floridian, *July 28, 1838. Courtesy of State Archives of Florida.*

Middle: From the census of 1855, Marion County, Florida. Alexander Casters was the owner of four slaves, two male and two female, who had a total value of $3,000 ($107,009 in 2025 dollars). *Courtesy of State Archives of Florida.*

Left: An auction announcement for the cash sale of enslaved human beings (referred to as "negroes; Boys, Men and one Woman") at the courthouse in Jacksonville, February 8, 1856. *Courtesy of State Archives of Florida.*

SLAVERY DURING THE CONFEDERACY (1861–65)

On February 8, 1861, seven states, including Florida, which had seceded from the United States, formed the Confederate States of America. The foundation of the Confederacy was chattel slavery, and slave labor was the cornerstone of its American Civil War effort. The Confederacy depended on slaves to provide labor for agriculture, railroading, infrastructure, fortifications and industrial enterprises. Slave labor was a major factor that allowed White men to serve in the Confederacy's military.

THE END OF SLAVERY IN THE UNITED STATES

After Confederate General Robert E. Lee surrendered to Union General Ulysses S. Grant at Appomattox Court House, Virginia, on April 9, 1865, the collapse of the Confederacy and the end of the American Civil War were imminent. Slavery unofficially ended, as no proslavery governmental authority was left in power to enforce it.

In December 1865, the official end of slavery in the United States was ensured with the passing of the Thirteenth Amendment to the U.S. Constitution, which abolished slavery and involuntary servitude, except as punishment for a crime.

CHAPTER 9

FORT MOSE

COLONIAL AMERICA'S FIRST FREE BLACK TOWN

Starting in the late seventeenth century, some escaped Black slaves from the southern British colonies fled to St. Augustine in Spanish Florida to seek asylum and gain their freedom. Spanish Florida would assist escaped slaves in setting up workshops if they already had a trade or granting land for cultivation if they were farmers. Escaped slaves were paid for their labor and for the products and harvests they produced. Many escaped slaves were assisted along their arduous southward journey by Native Americans, a precursor to the Underground Railroad.

In 1738, Gracia Real de Santa Teresa de Mose, a fortified town also known as Fort Mose, was built north of St. Augustine. It housed more than one hundred Black people who had escaped from slavery in the southern British colonies. Fort Mose became colonial America's first free Black town.

According to British accounts from later years, the original Fort Mose was "four square with a flanker at each corner, banked with earth, having a ditch on all sides lined round with prickly royal and…a well and housing within a lookout."

The Black Spanish militia from Fort Mose was led by an African-born escaped Black slave named Captain Francisco Menéndez.

SIEGE OF ST. AUGUSTINE (BATTLE OF BLOODY MOSE)

During June and July 1740, British troops led by General James Oglethorpe (a member of the United Kingdom's Parliament and founder of the Province of Georgia) attacked St. Augustine in Spanish Florida. This assault was part of the War of Jenkins' Ear (1739–48), which was a conflict between Britain and Spain caused by tensions over access to economic markets in Spanish America and British colonial expansion in North America.

In September 1739, Oglethorpe began aggression against Spanish Florida when he persuaded Britain's Creek Indian allies to attack both Spanish citizens and Florida Indians.

In December 1739, Oglethorpe organized multiple military forces, including the British Forty-Second Regiment on Foot, colonial militias from the Carolinas and the Province of Georgia and various Indian tribes, including the Chickasaw, Creek Shawnee and Yuchi. His goal was the defeat and capture of the Spanish stronghold of St. Augustine.

In May 1740, Oglethorpe's four hundred troops captured the Spanish garrisons of Fort San Diego, Fort Picolotta, Fort San Francisco de Pupo and Fort Mose. Most of Fort Mose's residents fled to the safety of Castillo de San Marcos in St. Augustine.

On June 24, 1740, British naval ships blockaded the port of St. Augustine with the goal of starving its citizens. The siege of St. Augustine began as Oglethorpe ordered rigorous military bombardments that lasted for twenty-seven days.

On June 26, 1740, the Spanish launched a siege of Fort Mose (known as the Battle of Bloody Mose) with 300 soldiers consisting of Spanish militiamen, Native allies and free Blacks. The surprise attack killed 68 and captured 34 of the 120 British Highland Rangers and 30 Native allies that were stationed at the fort. Fort Mose was back under Spanish control, but it had suffered major structural damage.

Several Spanish blockade runners evaded the patrolling British naval vessels and landed supply ships to support St. Augustine's citizenry and soldiers. Knowing that the Spanish would not be starved into surrendering, Oglethorpe then planned a blitzkrieg, attacking St. Augustine by land while British naval ships engaged Spanish ships in and near the harbor.

After realizing it was hurricane season and still stinging from the defeat and heavy casualties sustained during the Battle of Bloody Mose, Oglethorpe discarded the blitzkrieg plan, abandoned much of his artillery and returned to the Province of Georgia.

Fort Mose was abandoned from 1740 until 1752. A second fort was built near the site of the first by the Spanish in 1752. The second Fort Mose was a larger, earthen-walled structure, surrounded by a moat on three sides and bordered by a river on its fourth side. It included several thatched huts and a

CAPTAIN FRANCISCO MENÉNDEZ (1704?–1763?)

Menéndez was most likely born in the Gambia region of West Africa sometime around 1704. He was captured as a boy in Africa and enslaved on a plantation in the British colony of Carolina. During the Yamasee War (1715–17), he and his wife, Ana Maria de Escobar, and others escaped and fled to Spanish Florida. In 1718, this group of Blacks was sold back into slavery in Spanish Florida to Francisco Menéndez Márquez and baptized Catholic. This is how Francisco Menéndez acquired his name. His original name is unknown.

In 1726, Francisco Menéndez was appointed captain of St. Augustine's Black militia, although he was still enslaved. Captain Menéndez participated in military raids against the British Carolina militia and in defense of St. Augustine. After becoming literate, he petitioned Spanish Florida Governor Manuel de Montiano for his freedom and that of thirty other escaped slaves. In 1738, Governor de Montiano granted freedom to them and to all other escaped slaves who would flee from British Carolina. Governor de Montiano also chartered the settlement of Fort Mose, and Captain Menéndez was instrumental in its establishment.

Fort Mose caused major tensions between the British and Spanish Florida. In 1740, British militia forces defeated Fort Mose. Captain Menéndez then became a Spanish privateer, and his ship was captured by the British in 1741. The British severely whipped and tortured him and sold him back into slavery in the Bahamas. In 1759, Menéndez returned to Florida (whether he escaped British slavery or was ransomed by the Spanish is not known). He assisted in the rebuilding of the second Fort Mose and was appointed its free commander. In 1763, the Seven Years' War ended, and Spain ceded Florida to the British. Menéndez and other former slaves feared being enslaved again, so they went along with most of the Spanish citizens in St. Augustine as they were evacuated to Cuba. Menéndez established a new community in Cuba called San Agustín de la Nueva Florida (St. Augustine of the New Florida). Eventually Menéndez sold his land and moved his family to Havana, where they received a pension from the Spanish government. The historical record is not clear as to when or where he died.

Model of the second Fort Mose in the visitor center at Fort Mose Historic State Park. *Photograph by author.*

Location of the original Fort Mose at Fort Mose Historic State Park. *Photograph by author.*

lookout tower. The fort remained a defensive garrison for the protection of St. Augustine until 1763, when Spanish Florida was ceded to the British at the end of the Seven Years' War.

In 1764, the British repurposed Fort Mose and held it until 1783, when Florida was ceded back to Spain after the American Revolutionary War.

During the Patriot's Rebellion (1812–14), Fort Mose was destroyed and abandoned. It was lost to history for more than a century. In 1986, it was rediscovered by the Fort Mose Research Team. Thermal imaging technology located the first fort, which now lies in a salt marsh. The second fort was located using aerial photographs and old maps. Archaeological excavations have discovered artifacts that have led to a better understanding of the fort's inhabitants and its historical importance.

On October 12, 1994, Fort Mose was designated a National Historic Landmark because it was the first legally sanctioned free Black community in what is now the United States.

CHAPTER 10

THE BRITISH PERIOD (1763–83)

During the Seven Years' War, a global armed conflict fought mainly in Europe and the Americas involving most of the European powers, the British captured the Spanish colonies of the Philippines and Cuba. After the war ended, Spain transferred Florida to the British in exchange for the Philippines and Cuba via the signing of the First Treaty of Paris on February 10, 1763.

BRITISH EAST AND WEST FLORIDA

Due to the size of Florida, its lack of adequate roadways and its rugged frontier landscape, the British divided Florida into two separate colonies: East Florida, with its capital located at St. Augustine, and West Florida, with its capital located at Pensacola.

The British colonial government began the monumental task of repopulating the Florida colonies and making them profitable. British officials invalidated a large number of fraudulent land claims that were unofficially signed by corrupt Spanish and British land agents before the British government gained legal title to Florida.

On November 15–18, 1765, the first Picolata Conference was held between British officials and a delegation of Lower Creek and Seminole Indian leaders to set the boundaries between Indian and British land. A treaty was signed, and the Indians ceded more than two million acres of land in northeast Florida in exchange for gifts. This gave the British legal title to a vast portion of former Indian lands.

The Spanish never properly surveyed Florida, especially the interior sections, so the British sent in surveyors to accurately measure and map the colonies. These accurate surveys were used to partition land parcels into governmental and private property.

Several policies were set up to encourage settlement in the British East and West Florida colonies. The Councils of East and West Florida offered land grants to British military veterans of the Seven Years' War. Any head of a household could apply for one hundred acres for himself and fifty acres for each additional family member. Over 1.4 million acres were titled to investment organizations and the British nobility, with the provision that they would recruit settlers onto the land within a set period of time.

Mainly due to geography, East Florida prospered significantly more than West Florida. There were 2.86 million acres of land granted in East Florida, compared to only 380,000 acres granted in West Florida. Settlers in East Florida were primarily Europeans and Southern planters who recognized the area as part of the Atlantic coastal plain and established many large-scale plantations in its fertile regions. West Florida proved difficult to develop even though it had the towns of Mobile, Natchez and Pensacola. Its settlers were primarily European pioneers who relocated

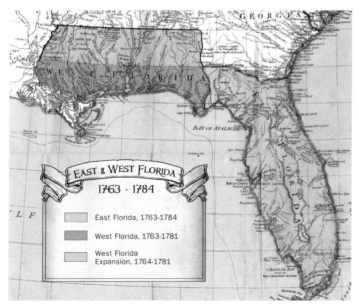

Map of British East and West Florida, 1763–84. *Author's collection.*

Ruins of the Three Chimneys sugar mill and rum distillery in Ormond Beach. Richard Oswald had it built by Black slaves in 1765–68 after receiving a British land grant awarded by King George III. *Courtesy of Ormond Beach Historical Society.*

from other British colonies to the north, mainly scantly populated Alabama and the western section of Georgia.

East Florida's Governor James Grant aggressively promoted his colony as "Britannia's New Eden." British planters cultivated cash crops including cotton, indigo, rice, sugar and timber. They also produced products such as naval stores (liquid products including rosin, tall oil, pine oil and turpentine), rum and silk. Since the British plantation labor system was based on chattel slavery, the demographics of the colony dramatically changed as large numbers of Black slaves were imported from Africa. Blacks actually outnumbered Whites for much of the British period in Florida.

KINGS ROAD

In order to entice settlers into Florida and promote trade with other colonies, the British made plans to construct a new major road. Started in 1766, Kings Road was scouted by a Creek Indian; financed by a combination of the British government and land and plantation owners; and built mainly by slave labor. Completed in 1775, Kings Road was 126 miles long and stretched from the St. Mary's River to New Smyrna. Its northern section connected with another road that led to Savannah, Georgia.

For almost one hundred years, Kings Road was the main land transportation link that connected Florida with the rest of the United States.

THE AMERICAN REVOLUTIONARY WAR (1775–83)

In 1775, the American Revolutionary War began. On July 4, 1776, thirteen colonies (Connecticut, Delaware, Georgia, Massachusetts, Maryland, New Hampshire, New Jersey, New York, North Carolina, Pennsylvania, Rhode Island, South Carolina and Virginia) signed the Declaration of Independence, which defined them as sovereign states that were no longer subject to British colonial rule. The East and West Florida colonies remained loyal to Britain's King George III and became a haven for British Loyalists.

When British Loyalists fled to the Florida colonies, they brought their Black slaves with them. By 1783, the population of East Florida was recorded as 11,285 slaves and only 6,090 Whites. This influx of people boosted Florida's economy as British Loyalists, Indians and slaves provided significant amounts of agricultural products to the British war effort.

THE LAST NAVAL BATTLE OF THE AMERICAN REVOLUTIONARY WAR

The Last Naval Battle of the American Revolutionary War Marker, located on Merritt Island, reads:

The last naval battle of the American Revolutionary War took place off the coast of Cape Canaveral on March 10, 1783. The fight began when three British ships sighted two Continental Navy ships, the Alliance commanded by Captain John Barry and the Duc De Lauzun commanded by Captain John Green sailing northward along the coast of Florida. The Alliance, a 36-gun frigate, and the Duc De Lauzun, a 20-gun ship, were loaded with 72,000 Spanish silver dollars they were bringing from Havana, Cuba to Philadelphia to support the Continental Army. One of the British ships, the HMS Sybil, a 28-gun frigate, commanded by Captain James Vashon, chased the Alliance and Duc De Lauzun to the south. The HMS Sybil fired first, exchanging shots with the slower Duc De Lauzun. Then in a daring strategy Captain John Barry aboard the Alliance reversed his course, and while under fire, waited until the HMS Sybil was close. When the British ship was alongside he returned fire to the broadside with greater number of cannon. The battle lasted less than an hour, when the HMS Sybil, outgunned and badly damaged, broke off from the battle and fled. The Alliance and Duc De Lauzun then continued on their mission at dawn on March 11, 1783.

Spain joined the American Revolutionary War as an ally of the United States and declared war on Great Britain in 1779. The Spanish concentrated on attacks against the British in the Gulf of Mexico. In 1780, Spain captured and occupied Mobile. In 1781, Spain defeated British forces in Pensacola, which effectively handed the Spanish control and possession of West Florida.

In October 1781, the British were decisively defeated in the Battle of Yorktown in Virginia, which effectively ended the American Revolutionary War. On September 3, 1783, the Treaty of Paris was signed, which officially ended the war and recognized the United States as a free, sovereign and independent nation.

Many people living in Florida expected the colony to become part of the newly created United States. However, Florida was transferred back to Spain. Most of the British citizens and Loyalists living in Florida moved to England or to British colonies in the Caribbean. Florida's Second Spanish Period began with the Spanish government struggling to administer, populate and protect the colony.

CHAPTER 11

DR. ANDREW TURNBULL
AND THE NEW SMYRNA COLONY

In 1768, Dr. Andrew Turnbull, a Scottish diplomat and physician, founded the colony of New Smyrna, which was located in British East Florida about sixty miles south of St. Augustine. The central part of the original colony can be found in what is now the downtown area of New Smyrna Beach. Turnbull named the colony in honor of the Greek city of Smyrna (his wife's birthplace). It was the largest British settlement in North America from 1768 to 1777.

The British government was desperate to develop its new East and West Florida colonies and authorized large land grants and bounty money for planters who could establish agricultural plantations that could produce in-demand goods such as cotton, indigo and silk.

In 1766 and 1767, the English government awarded twenty-thousand-acre land grants to Turnbull, Sir William Duncan and Sir Richard Temple, who envisioned business partnership opportunities in East Florida. Turnbull traveled south of St. Augustine to locate an area to set up a colony on what was then unclaimed British property. Entering Mosquito Inlet (now Ponce de Leon Inlet), he located an ideal and attractive area with many magnolia, live oak and bay trees. This was the area he selected to build his New Smyrna colony.

Turnbull returned to England to request more land from the British government, as his plans for the New Smyrna colony were much larger than his original twenty-thousand-acre land grant could sustain. British governmental officials were very receptive to his ideas and they granted him more land and provided funding to recruit colonists and build much-needed infrastructure.

During the spring of 1767, Turnbull voyaged to the Mediterranean Sea to recruit workers from Greece. He believed Greek laborers would be able to adapt to Florida's heat and humidity. He encountered interference from Ottoman Empire officials in Greece and failed to recruit enough colonists. He then traveled to southern Italy and Minorca. Due to significant crop failures on the island of Minorca over the previous three years, Turnbull was able to recruit a large number of Minorcans, many of whom were farmers. He secured about 1,400 colonists in total, which included 1,100 from Minorca, 200 from Greece and about 100 from the countries of Corsica, France, Italy and Turkey. These colonists were placed under contract as indentured servants, and their agreement stated they were required to labor at the New Smyrna colony for a number of years and then either be given ship passage back to their homeland or awarded a plot of land in British East Florida.

Portrait of Dr. Andrew Turnbull. *Courtesy of State Archives of Florida.*

On April 17, 1768, Turnbull set sail for East Florida with eight ships carrying the 1,400 colonists. During the four-month voyage, many colonists experienced serious health conditions, mainly scurvy and infections, which killed about 150 of the ships' passengers.

GOOD TIMES AND BAD TIMES

From 1768 to 1771, Turnbull's colonists, with the assistance of some Black slaves, managed to clear land, build housing, cultivate agricultural fields and construct supporting buildings and infrastructure for the plantation. However, harsh Florida environmental conditions coupled with brutal working conditions and poor nutrition led to many deaths.

From 1771 to 1773, crop yields, working conditions and living standards improved, as did the health of the colonists, and the death rate was reduced.

Postcard titled "Historic Old Fort Ruins—New Smyrna Beach," circa 1960s. These ruins are reportedly the coquina rock foundation of a warehouse building that once served the New Smyrna Colony. The structure was built by Andrew Turnbull around 1770 on top of a Native American shell mound. *Author's collection.*

Droughts in 1773 and 1775 drastically reduced crop yields and caused food shortages, which led to increased deaths among the colonists.

After 1775, weather conditions improved, and crop yields of corn, hemp, indigo, rice and sugar increased. However, the colonists began voicing concerns that Turnbull would not honor their contracts and complained about poor working conditions, especially the harsh treatment they were enduring from his overseers. Safety concerns regarding skirmishes with Native Indians, which caused injuries and several colonists' deaths, were also a cause of uneasiness.

THE COLONY'S DOWNFALL

In 1777, Turnbull's colonists, the vast majority Minorcans, revolted and marched north to St. Augustine to discuss their fate with East Florida Governor Patrick Tonyn. The colonists were granted asylum in St. Augustine, and Governor Tonyn also awarded them a small section of the walled town to live in.

Patrick Tonyn, the third and last governor of British East Florida (who served from 1774 to 1783). *Courtesy of Wikimedia Commons.*

Turnbull could not produce enough marketable crops at the New Smyrna Colony and lost the support of the British government, as well as his investors. The New Smyrna Colony was forced to cease most of its plantation operations and was virtually abandoned.

In 1783, after Spain regained control of Florida, Turnbull left his plantation house at the New Smyrna Colony and retired in Charleston, South Carolina, where he died on March 13, 1792.

CHAPTER 12

THE PATRIOTS REBELLION (1812–14)

The Patriots Rebellion (sometimes referred to as the Patriot War) was an armed conflict that occurred in Spanish East Florida before and during the War of 1812. The United States unwisely, illegally and clandestinely supported insurrectionists from Georgia as they attempted to incite a revolt to subvert Spanish rule in East Florida and seize the geographically important territory. The conflict evolved into a bloodbath of ambushes and scorched-earth warfare tactics in which many plantations and farmsteads from the Georgia border to south of St. Augustine were looted or set aflame. Supporters of the United States' quest to seize East Florida stated they wanted to limit British influence in North America, stop smuggling and prevent military deserters and runaway slaves from seeking asylum in the Spanish territory.

Since the Patriots Rebellion was fought on a regional scale, did not include any legendary or charismatic generals or fabled battles and has been overshadowed by the War of 1812, it has been virtually forgotten in U.S. history.

The fourth president of the United States, James Madison, and his Secretary of State, James Monroe, secretly plotted to secure Spanish East Florida as a territory of the United States, fearing it would fall under British or French rule.

On January 15, 1811, Congress passed a secret act in closed session for acquisition of the area called the No-Transfer Resolution. This act, which opposed the transfer of territories from one European power to another

Portrait of James Madison, fourth president of the United States, circa 1816. *Courtesy of Wikimedia Commons.*

in the Western Hemisphere, was the U.S. government's first statement regarding its own security. The No-Transfer Resolution established a formal U.S. policy toward the government's goals of seizing Spanish borderlands.

Madison appointed former governor of Georgia General George Mathews as a clandestine government agent. Mathews then led a contingent of militia forces (primarily made up of disloyal Spanish subjects and volunteers from

Georgia and Tennessee who were promised two hundred acres of Florida land in return for their service). This group of militia forces became known as the Patriots and declared themselves in a revolt against Spain.

THE "PATRIOTS" INVADE SPANISH EAST FLORIDA

President Madison ordered U.S. forces (including U.S. Navy gunboats, riflemen, infantry and marine troops) to cross the international border into East Florida to support local revolts against what was falsely deemed Spanish oppression. A guerrilla war in East Florida ensued in which thousands of people were killed or injured, residential and commercial property was looted and destroyed, crops were decimated and livestock was killed, run off or stolen, leading to food shortages. Terroristic scorched-earth tactics were utilized.

On March 17, 1812, the Patriots seized Fernandina, raised their flag and offered the land to U.S. Colonel Smith, who accepted it on behalf of the United States. Soon afterward, the insurgents established a republic with a constitution that included a court system, an executive office and a legislative council called the Republic of East Florida. John Houston McIntosh, a wealthy planter and politician from Georgia, served as its first president.

Patriot forces then marched toward St. Augustine and set up headquarters at Fort Mose. The Patriot forces could not gather enough support from local citizens and did not have the strength to seize the fortified city of St. Augustine.

SALUS POPULI LEX SUPREMA

Flag of the Republic of East Florida. The Latin phrase *Salus populi lex suprema* translates to "The safety of the people is the supreme law." *Courtesy of Wikimedia Commons.*

THE WAR OF 1812 BEGINS

On June 16, 1812, the War of 1812 began between the United States and England and their distinct allies. The United States found itself in an awkward position militarily and politically regarding the Patriots Rebellion. The young nation was not prepared, militarily or politically, to continue supporting the unprovoked invasion of Spanish East Florida but believed keeping troops there would guard against potential British invasion from its southern borders.

U.S. public support of the Patriots Rebellion dissolved, and Madison's opponents condemned the insurrection, stating the reasons for the invasion of Spanish East Florida were both ill-advised and unethical.

MADISON SEVERS U.S. SUPPORT FOR THE "PATRIOTS"

President Madison perceived the public dissatisfaction and diplomatic uneasiness over his support of the Patriots Rebellion and feared that Spain might ally with Britain against the United States in the War of 1812. Madison decided to halt U.S. support for the Patriots Rebellion.

On April 4, 1812, Secretary of State James Monroe sent a letter to George Mathews stating that the U.S. government did not approve of the methods he used to seize Amelia Island and other areas of East Florida as they were "not authorized by the law of the United States, or the instructions founded on it." Mathews was abruptly replaced by David Mitchell, the governor of Georgia.

The Seminoles and their Black allies joined forces with the Spanish government and successfully ambushed several companies of Patriot militiamen, which further weakened the Republic of East Florida.

In January 1814, a group of Patriot militiamen and settlers erected a twenty-five-square-foot blockhouse called Fort Mitchell, which was most likely located in present-day Alachua County, and declared it to be the capital of the Republic of East Florida. General Buckner F. Harris, director of the Republic of East Florida, petitioned the U.S. government to annex this land from the Spanish. Secretary of State James Monroe answered and made it clear that the Patriot government was not supported or recognized by the U.S. government.

THE PATRIOTS REBELLION ENDS

On May 5, 1814, the Seminoles ambushed, killed and scalped Buckner F. Harris. The Seminoles presented Spanish East Florida's governor, Sebastián Kindelán y O'Regan, with Harris's scalp. Governor O'Regan promptly paid the Seminoles a bounty reward for killing Harris.

After the death of Harris, their main leader, and with no support from the U.S. government, the Patriots Rebellion was extinguished in Spanish East Florida.

CONSEQUENCES OF THE PATRIOTS REBELLION IN U.S. HISTORY

The Patriots Rebellion was a military and political debacle that was both embarrassing to the Madison administration within the United States and internationally discreditable to early U.S. foreign policy. The Madison administration allowed filibusters (nineteenth-century irregular military adventurers who claimed to be acting on behalf of U.S. interests while seeking out and engaging in conflicts with nations with which the United States was at peace) to exploit boundary disputes between East Florida and Georgia. Common sense, ethics and the truth were sacrificed under the pretense of national security.

It is important to realize that the political and military strategies of the Patriots Rebellion, disgraceful and otherwise, helped lay the groundwork for continued and long-lasting U.S. policies associated with international affairs, expansionist politics (efforts to seize as much land as possible in North America), the continued enslavement of Black people and discrimination against and displacement of Native Americans.

CHAPTER 13

THE THREE SEMINOLE WARS

WHO ARE THE SEMINOLE INDIANS?

The Seminole Indians are the descendants of Creek and other Indigenous groups who moved into Florida starting in the 1700s and continuing into the 1800s from what is now Alabama and Georgia. By that time, the ravages of European colonization had devastated the Timucua, the Apalachee and other Native American groups. Some of the survivors likely joined the Creeks and other newcomers. By the second half of the 1700s, these Natives had become known as Seminoles (a derivative of the Spanish word *cimarrón*, which means "wild," "runaway" or, perhaps, "people who had left their traditional lands").

During the period from 1816 to 1858, there were three Seminole wars that pitted U.S. soldiers and militiamen against Native Americans. These conflicts (mainly the First and Second Seminole Wars) were the only Indian wars in U.S. history in which slavery played an important role. The wars attracted national attention, obstructed territorial progress and delayed Florida's aspirations to statehood. As a result of these wars, the majority of the Seminole people were forcibly moved to Indian Territory west of the Mississippi River. The resettlement opened former Seminole lands to Whites.

THE FIRST SEMINOLE WAR (1816–19)

In the early 1800s, Seminole Indians, Black Seminoles, freed Black people and runaway Black slaves were living in the northern regions of Spanish Florida. Border tensions between Spanish Florida and southern U.S. states were escalating as armed attacks and skirmishes between the adversaries were becoming more frequent.

On July 27, 1816, U.S. General Andrew Jackson ordered General Edmund Gaines to invade Spanish Florida, destroy British-built Negro Fort near present-day Apalachicola and return all escaped slaves to their owners. During the Battle of Negro Fort, U.S. cannon fire exploded in the ammunition storage area, destroying the fort. More than 200 of the 334 escaped slaves living in the fort were killed. Survivors fled south.

GENERAL ANDREW JACKSON ASSAILED AS A TYRANT AND MURDERER

When General Jackson arrived in St. Marks, he ordered the execution by hanging of two captured Indian leaders, Josiah Francis and Hoemotchernucho, without a trial. Many in Europe and elsewhere considered this an act of barbarity and a flagrant violation of the conventions of warfare. Jackson then captured two British subjects: Alexander Arbuthnot, a seventy-year-old Scottish merchant and translator, and Robert Ambrister, a Royal Navy veteran. A U.S. military court found them guilty of espionage and aiding the enemy and ordered them executed. Soon afterward, the officers of the military court commuted Ambrister's death sentence, but Jackson promptly overruled them. On April 29, 1818, Arbuthnot was hanged from the masthead of a schooner and Ambrister was shot dead by a firing squad. Jackson used these executions to blame Indians and outside agitators for creating problems for the U.S. government and to justify U.S. military invasions into Spanish Florida. The executions were met with considerable international protest, especially from the British and Spanish governments, which assailed Jackson as a tyrant and murderer. The U.S. Congress opened an investigation and actually condemned Jackson's actions. However, Jackson did not receive any formal punishment. In 1821, Jackson was appointed federal military commissioner (governor) of Florida by President Monroe. In 1829, Jackson became the seventh president of the United States.

In November 1817, the Mikasukis Indian village of Fowltown (near present-day Bainbridge, Georgia) was attacked by U.S. forces. The former Creek Indian agent and governor of Georgia David Brydie Mitchell declared this attack the beginning of the First Seminole War. Soon afterward, a group of Seminole warriors attacked a boat on the Apalachicola River heading to Fort Scott, killing forty-three people.

In December 1817, General Andrew Jackson led invasions along the Suwannee River and Lake Miccosukee and destroyed several Seminole villages. Jackson also seized the Spanish military post at St. Marks, assisted by U.S. naval support. Jackson's forces also temporarily occupied Pensacola.

Jackson's invasions made it clear to the Spanish government that they did not have the resources or military power to combat local uprisings or protect Florida against U.S. aggression.

In 1819, the Adams-Onís Treaty was signed ceding Spanish Florida to the United States. The official transfer took place in 1821.

THE SECOND SEMINOLE WAR (1835–42)

In 1823, the Treaty of Moultrie Creek was signed by the government of the United States and the chiefs of several Indian bands in Florida. The treaty established a Seminole reservation in the center of the Florida peninsula.

In May 1832, a small number of Seminoles signed the Treaty of Payne's Landing, raising tensions with other chiefs and tribal leaders. The treaty stated that the Seminole people had three years to cede their land to the U.S. government and relocate to Indian Territory. Some Seminoles did relocate, but many refused to obey the treaty and stayed in Florida.

The Indian Removal Act of 1830 was signed into law by President Andrew Jackson. This U.S. law allowed the forced removal of Indian people from their rightful land and their relocation to a reservation in present-day Oklahoma. In Florida, this meant that all Seminoles were to be forced out of the territory. When Seminoles refused to relocate, U.S. Army troops began arriving to enforce the Indian Removal Act.

On December 28, 1835, about 180 Seminole warriors led by Alligator, Jumper and Micanopy ambushed 110 U.S. troops led by Major Francis Dade in present-day Sumter County. Only one U.S. soldier survived. Known as the Dade Massacre, the battle is considered the beginning of the Second Seminole War. The same day as the Dade Massacre, Indian Agent Wiley Thompson and six others were ambushed and killed near Fort King,

An 1831 Florida map displaying the Seminole Indian Reservation in the central part of the territory. *Author's collection.*

present-day Ocala, by a band of Seminole warriors led by Osceola, the well-known Seminole war leader.

With less than three thousand warriors and no way to replace their losses, the Seminoles engaged in guerrilla warfare against more than forty thousand troops and militiamen over seven years. When U.S. forces were unable to win the war on the battlefield, questionable tactics were used. General Zachary Taylor, who later served as the twelfth president of the United States, brought in bloodhounds to hunt down Native Americans.

General Thomas Jesup ordered Osceola to be captured under a white flag of truce. Osceola was transferred to Fort Moultrie, near Charleston, where he died in captivity. The U.S. government authorized Brigadier General Walker Keith Armistead to offer bribes to Seminole chiefs in order to get them to surrender and move west.

In August 1842, several Seminole chiefs met at the U.S. Army's headquarters in Cedar Keys. Each Seminole was offered a rifle, ammunition, money and one year's rations if they moved west. Most opted to stay in Florida.

Osceola, the famous Seminole war leader. Portrait by George Catlin, circa 1838. *Courtesy of Wikimedia Commons.*

On August 14, 1842, Colonel William Jenkins Worth declared the Second Seminole War to be over, even though there was no treaty of peace signed or any official documented end to the war. Some Seminoles were allowed to live in an informal reservation in southwestern Florida instead of being relocated to Indian territory.

Estimates of the monetary costs of the Second Seminole War range from $30 million to $40 million ($1.15 billion to $1.54 billion in 2025 dollars). The number of U.S. Army, Navy and Marine regulars who served in Florida is listed in military records as 10,169. About 30,000 militiamen and volunteers also served in the war for the United States.

The U.S. Army officially recorded 1,466 deaths (215 were officers), mostly from disease. The number killed in action is not clear. The U.S. Navy and Marine Corps estimated 69 deaths, but that number is not accurate, as many of the wounded and sick were sent out of Florida and some died elsewhere.

The number of White civilians, Seminoles and Black Seminoles killed is uncertain, as no accurate records documenting those numbers, or the numbers of those who died of starvation or other privations caused by the war, have ever been gathered.

By the end of 1843, the United States had managed to ship 3,824 Native Americans and several hundred Black Seminoles from Florida to Indian Territory (present-day Oklahoma).

The Second Seminole War was the costliest, deadliest and longest of all Indian wars in U.S. history.

THE THIRD SEMINOLE WAR (1855–58)

In 1855, the Third Seminole War broke out. Concentrated in southwest Florida and the Everglades, it was caused by Whites intruding into Seminole lands. The Seminoles, with a population of only about three hundred, again used guerrilla warfare against U.S. troops and militiamen, who were, yet again, unprepared for such tactics.

In June 1856, a battle broke out at the Tillis family farm near Fort Meade in which two White settlers and several Seminoles were killed, including Oscen Tustenuggee, the prime war chief of the Seminoles. Afterward, the Seminoles retreated farther south into the Everglades.

U.S. troops and militiamen commanded by General William S. Harney invaded the Everglades, scattering families and burning crops. When Seminoles, including women and children, were captured, they were forcibly relocated west to Indian Territory.

The next year, larger numbers of U.S. troops and militiamen again destroyed Indian villages and crops. Few Seminole warriors were killed or captured, but the Indians were facing starvation.

In March 1858, the Seminole's most prominent chief, Billy Bowlegs, finally met with White U.S. officials and Seminoles who were brought from Arkansas to Florida to assist in peace negotiations. Most of the Florida Seminoles followed by Billy Bowlegs agreed to be relocated to Indian Territory, effectively ending the war. At least 150 Seminoles remained in Florida, and many of their descendants are still living in the state today.

None of the three Seminole Wars were ended by official acts of surrender or signed peace treaties.

CHAPTER 14

THE SECOND SPANISH PERIOD, U.S. TERRITORY AND STATEHOOD

SPAIN REGAINS POSSESSION OF FLORIDA IN 1783

In 1783, the American Revolutionary War officially came to an end with the signing of the Treaties of Versailles, part of the Peace of Paris. Spain regained possession of East and West Florida from the British. Many British subjects moved from Florida to British colonies in the Caribbean. The Second Spanish Period was a frontier struggle for power, money and resources (including slaves) between Spanish, English, Indian (Cherokees, Chickasaws, Choctaws, Creeks and Seminoles) and the U.S., these factions did not trust one another.

In 1784, Vicente Manuel de Céspedes, East Florida's governor, arrived in St. Augustine with five hundred troops and several hundred civil staff and their families to find the city in a fairly distressed condition. Less than three hundred homes were standing, only about half of them in good condition. The monastery had been converted into a barracks, the hospital-church of La Soledad was a pile of rubble and the wooden barracks built by the British had been burned to the ground.

Governor de Céspedes quickly realized that Spanish Florida was in a weak and vulnerable predicament. He knew recruiting more settlers and forming alliances with Native Americans and traders were required in order to establish an efficient colony. He initially wanted to restrict the residents of East Florida to Spanish and non-Spanish Catholics.

Spanish King Charles III created this Spanish national flag in 1785. It flew over Spanish Florida until the United States took official possession of the territory in 1821. *Courtesy of Florida Department of State.*

To entice settlers and businessmen into Spanish Florida, large land grants were offered by the Spanish Crown. Additionally, offers such as ten years of tax-free occupancy and cash bonuses to start farms were tendered. By 1786, Governor de Céspedes had realized that not only were Englishmen and other non-Catholics needed to strengthen the colony but that they also were not going to convert to Catholicism, so he dropped the Catholicism requirement. Slave owners were also permitted to migrate into Spanish Florida, which created fear and tension among free Black people and escaped slaves living within the colony.

Throughout the Second Spanish Period, problems along the Georgia-Florida border continued, with raiders entering Florida, stealing slaves and rustling cattle. Military uprisings such as the Patriots Rebellion and the First Seminole War proved that Spain did not have the military power or monetary resources to protect or retain Spanish Florida. With the United States gaining population, resources and military power, Spain had little choice but to cede its Florida colonies to the United States.

In 1819, the Adams-Onís Treaty transferred the Spanish Florida territories to the United States. In 1821, Florida officially became a U.S. territory.

THE UNITED STATES TAKES POSSESSION OF FLORIDA IN 1821

On March 12, 1821, Secretary of State John Quincy Adams appointed General Andrew Jackson military governor of the U.S. Territory of Florida. Jackson was tasked with settling land claims from both British and Spanish titles and transferring Spanish property to the many colonists migrating into the territory from parts of the United States. Most Spanish, Indians and Blacks disliked Jackson and were wary of the decisions he would make regarding their futures. Many Spanish subjects decided to flee Florida; several burned their homes to the ground before they left.

Seal of the Territory of Florida (1821–45). *Courtesy of Wikimedia Commons.*

On November 12, 1821, Jackson resigned from his position as military governor of Florida and returned to Tennessee with aspirations to run for president of the United States.

East and West Florida were merged into one entity, and in 1824, Tallahassee was established as the capital of the U.S. Territory of Florida. The former East Florida became St. Johns County, and the former West Florida became Escambia County.

Florida's financial problems during the territorial period hampered its efforts to build roads and improve transportation into the interior areas and northward into U.S. states, which many considered its main issue. The territory had limited revenue, mainly consisting of taxes on land sales, license fees and election poll taxes. Two political factions were in contention regarding territorial development: the Whigs and the Democrats. The Whigs wanted to increase spending using public funds for railroads and state banks. They were supported by large plantation owners and led by Richard Keith Call, an attorney, politician, slave owner and member of the Florida Territorial Council. The Democrats wanted less spending of public funds and lower taxes. They were supported by frontiersmen and small farmers and led by David Levy Yulee, an attorney, politician, slave owner and senator representing Florida. Yulee is known as the "Father of Florida Railroads."

The issue of statehood was also argued by differing political interests. Some wanted statehood for the entire territory, others separate statehood for East and West Florida. Other factions preferred Florida to remain a territory.

Governor's Name	Duration of Term(s)	Political Party	Appointed by U.S. President
William Pope Duval	April 17, 1822 to April 17, 1834	Democratic	James Monroe John Quincy Adams Andrew Jackson
John Eaton	April 24, 1834 to March 16, 1836	Democratic	Andrew Jackson
Richard K. Call	March 16, 1836 to December 2, 1839	Whig	Andrew Jackson Martin Van Buren
Robert R. Reid	December 12, 1839 to March 19, 1841	Democratic	Martin Van Buren
Richard K. Call	March 19, 1841 to August 11, 1844	Whig	William Henry Harrison John Tyler
John Branch	August 11, 1844 to June 25, 1845	Democratic	John Tyler

List of the six Territory of Florida governors.

At the Constitutional Convention of 1838, hosted in the town of St. Joseph, delegates from across the Territory of Florida gathered to establish a constitution in preparation for statehood. The approved constitution featured a bicameral legislature, a one-term governor, tight banking restrictions (due to the national banking crisis of 1837) and a strict separation of church and state (which stipulated that no clergyman could serve as governor or legislator).

Since Florida was a slaveholding territory, the U.S. Congress would not approve its admission to the Union until a non-slaveholding territory was eligible. In 1845, Iowa, a non-slaveholding territory, was admitted to the Union.

FLORIDA BECOMES THE TWENTY-SEVENTH STATE IN 1845

On March 3, 1845, President Tyler signed legislation admitting Florida into the Union as the twenty-seventh state. Florida's State Legislative Council organized the first state election. A state governor, a member of the U.S. Congress, seventeen state senators and forty-one state representatives were elected to office.

THE "LOST" TOWN OF ST. JOSEPH

Founded in 1835, the town of St. Joseph became something of a boomtown as it quickly developed into a prosperous shipping port. By 1837, St. Joseph had the largest population in the Territory of Florida. In 1841, a yellow fever epidemic led to the abandonment of the town. In 1844, the remnants of the town were destroyed and washed away by a storm surge. Today, nothing remains of the town of St. Joseph, and the original signed constitutional document from the Constitutional Convention of 1838 is also lost to history.

William D. Moseley, a plantation owner, was elected the state of Florida's first governor. David Levy Yulee, a staunch supporter of statehood, was elected U.S. senator.

The issue of slavery in the state of Florida became a main concern. Most eligible voters in Florida, White males, supported slavery. The five-county region (Gadsden, Leon, Jefferson, Madison and Hamilton Counties) of North Florida (known as Middle Florida) was home to many farms and plantations that primarily grew cotton. The economy of Middle Florida was based on slave labor, and most of Florida's Black slaves lived in this region. By 1850, Florida's population had grown to 87,445. Its Black slaves numbered about 39,000 (almost half the state's population at the time). There were also about 1,000 free Black people living in the state.

In 1860, the antislavery Republican Party's candidate, Abraham Lincoln, was elected president of the United States. A major national crisis began as slaveholding states felt their slavery-based plantation economy was under threat. Tensions between northern and southern states over slavery began to escalate to levels that threatened the stability of the nation.

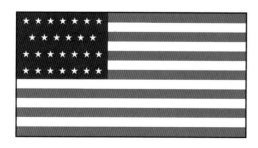

Flag of the United States in 1845 (twenty-seven stars) after Florida was granted statehood. *Courtesy of Wikimedia Commons.*

CHAPTER 15

SECESSION AND THE AMERICAN CIVIL WAR

At the South, and with our People of course, slavery is the element of all value,
and a destruction of that destroys all that is property.
—*President John C. McGehee, Florida Secession Convention*

FLORIDA SECEDES FROM THE UNION IN 1861

On January 3, 1861, a special secession convention began in Tallahassee with sixty-nine delegates, who were all White slave owners, to decide if Florida would secede from the Union. Madison Starke Perry, fourth governor of Florida, and governor-elect John Milton (lawyer and member of the Florida House of Representatives) were strong supporters of secession. The debate lasted about a week.

On January 10, 1861, a vote of sixty-two to seven decided that Florida would secede from the Union. Florida was the third state to secede (South Carolina and Mississippi preceded it).

Ordinance of Secession

We, the People of the State of Florida in Convention assembled, do solemnly ordain, publish and declare: That the State of Florida hereby withdraws herself from the Confederacy of States existing under the name of the United States of America, and from the existing Government of said States; and that all political connection between her and the Government of said States ought to be and the same is hereby totally annulled, and said union of States dissolved; and the State of Florida is hereby declared a Sovereign and Independent Nation; and that all ordinances heretofore adopted in so far as they create or recognize said Union are rescinded; and all laws or parts of laws in force in this State, in so far as they recognize or assent to said Union be and they are hereby repealed.

Done in open Convention, January 10th, A.D. 1861.

On February 28, 1861, Florida joined the Confederate States of America (a proslavery government). Eleven states became members of the Confederacy: Alabama, Arkansas, Florida, Georgia, Louisiana, Mississippi, North Carolina, South Carolina, Tennessee, Texas and Virginia.

FLORIDA'S ROLE IN THE AMERICAN CIVIL WAR

On April 12, 1861, Confederate troops attacked the Union garrison of Fort Sumter in South Carolina. This event marked the beginning of the American Civil War, the costliest and deadliest war ever fought in North America.

An estimated fifteen thousand troops from Florida fought for the Confederacy. More than two thousand Whites and Blacks from Florida fought for the Union. Florida's main role in the war was as a source of food and supplies, including cattle, cotton, lumber, pork and salt. Crucial war materials and other supplies coming from the Bahamas, Bermuda and Cuba were transported in and out of Florida's many bays and inlets by blockade runners, many proficient at eluding the Union's navy.

Flag of Florida adopted during the American Civil War, designed by Confederate General Edward A. Perry in 1861. *Courtesy of Wikimedia Commons.*

NOTABLE BATTLES FOUGHT IN FLORIDA

Battle of Santa Rosa Island (October 9, 1861): Confederate forces attempted to capture Union-held Fort Pickens. The Union received reinforcements, which led them to victory. There were sixty-seven Union and eighty-seven Confederate casualties.

Yankee Outrage at Tampa (June 30–July 1, 1862): The USS *Sagamore*, a Union gunboat, opened fire and demanded Confederate forces surrender. A Confederate artillery company returned fire. There was no surrender, and the USS *Sagamore* sailed away. No casualties were reported from the skirmish.

Battle of St. Johns Bluff (October 1–3, 1862): Confederate forces attempted to stop Union ships from seizing control of the St. Johns River and Jacksonville. Union forces outmaneuvered the Confederates, which caused their withdrawal. The Union victory secured control of the Jacksonville area. No casualties were reported from this battle.

Battle of Fort Brooke (October 16–18, 1863): Two Union ships bombarded Fort Brooke as a landing party captured two Confederate blockade-running ships. Confederates destroyed a steamer ship to prevent it from being captured. The battle resulted in a Union victory. There were sixteen Confederate casualties and none reported by the Union.

Battle of Olustee (February 20, 1864): This battle was by far the largest fought in Florida. A Union expedition of 5,500 troops entered Florida to cut off Confederate supply routes and recruit Black soldiers. Initially, they met little resistance as they occupied and destroyed parts of the state and liberated Black slaves during their march. Union General Truman Seymour did not expect to encounter Confederate reinforcements from Charleston as he marched toward Tallahassee. Confederate General Joseph Finegan positioned 5,000 Confederate troops near Olustee Station. A furious battle broke out, and the Union forces retreated and fled to Jacksonville. The result of the battle was a Confederate victory: Union forces suffered 203 killed, 1,152 wounded and 506 missing for a total of 1,861 casualties, which was about 34 percent of the 5,500 Union troops. Confederate forces suffered 93 killed, 848 wounded and 8 captured or missing. The ratio of casualties to the number of troops involved made this battle the second bloodiest of the American Civil War for the Union, even though it was fought in the militarily insignificant state of Florida.

Battle of Natural Bridge (March 6, 1865): A joint Union expedition of seven hundred troops was searching for Confederate troops who had attacked Union facilities at Cedar Keys and Fort Meyers. These Confederate troops

American Civil War cannon at the Olustee Battlefield. *Photograph by author.*

were reportedly quartered near St. Marks. The Union troops attempted to cross Natural Bridge, and Confederate forces, one thousand strong, successfully repelled their advancement. The battle resulted in a Confederate victory. Both sides suffered some casualties. Twenty-one Union troops were killed, eighty-nine wounded and thirty-eight captured; three Confederates were killed and twenty-three wounded.

During the American Civil War, Florida was militarily insignificant and did not suffer much damage. The Union occupied many coastal towns and forts and possessed naval superiority; however, the interior sections of the state were controlled by the Confederacy.

THE AMERICAN CIVIL WAR ENDS

On April 9, 1865, Confederate General Robert E. Lee surrendered to Union General Ulysses S. Grant at Appomattox Court House, Virginia. This was the beginning of the end of the American Civil War.

More than 2.8 million men and a few hundred women served, and 618,222 were killed (360,222 Union and 258,000 Confederates). Of the 15,000 Floridians who fought for the Confederacy, about 5,000 died (a high

THE "MYSTERIOUS" DEATH OF FLORIDA GOVERNOR JOHN MILTON

In October 1861, John Milton became governor of Florida. He was a staunch supporter of secession and remained in office for the majority of the American Civil War. As it became clear that the Confederacy was going to be defeated, he remarked to the Florida legislature, "The Northern Army leaders have developed a character so odious that death would be preferable to reunion with them." On April 1, 1865, while still in office, he was found dead with a gunshot wound in his head. His family and church reported his death as an accident; however, many others believed he committed suicide, especially since he made public comments to that effect.

casualty rate of about 33 percent). It is estimated that at least 50,000 U.S. and Confederate civilians died as a result of the war; however, the actual number has never been confirmed.

RECONSTRUCTION IN FLORIDA

The end of the Civil War left the state of Florida economically depressed. Most of its economy was reliant on slavery, which was now abolished, and Confederate currency was valueless. Many plantations were sold to investors and broken up into smaller farms where sharecropping and tenant farming was implemented, oftentimes staffed by former slaves. The Freedman's Bureau was created to assist former slaves with employment, education and protection of their newly established citizenship rights.

In 1865 and 1866, former Confederate states including Florida passed laws called Black Codes that restricted the rights of Black people to own property, buy or lease land, conduct business and move freely in public spaces and ensured they would work for low or no wages.

The Thirteenth Amendment to the U.S. Constitution was passed in December 1865, abolishing slavery and involuntary servitude, except as punishment for a crime.

The U.S. Congress was controlled by the Radical Republicans, who did not agree with President Andrew Johnson's handling of Reconstruction.

Currency of the Confederate States of America: one-dollar bill issued by the State of Florida on March 1, 1863. *Photograph by author.*

The Reconstruction Acts of 1867–68 were passed, and the era of Radical Reconstruction began. Federal troops were stationed in the former Confederate states to administer the creation of democratic state governments until they complied with the federal government's readmission requirements.

Two other Reconstruction-era amendments to the U.S. Constitution were passed. The Fourteenth Amendment, ratified in 1868, granted citizenship to all people born in the United States and included the due process and equal protection clauses. This amendment was specifically designed to protect the rights of former slaves. The Fifteenth Amendment, ratified in 1870, granted Black men the right to vote.

After Florida agreed to register all its eligible voters, including Black people, and approve a new state constitution (which recognized the abolition of slavery and the right to equal protection under the law regardless of race or color), it was officially readmitted to the United States on June 25, 1868.

Thousands of Black men voted in Florida for the first time in their lives, which resulted in the election of Jonathan Clarkson Gibbs, Florida's first Black secretary of state (served from 1868 to 1872), and Josiah Thomas Walls, Florida's first Black congressman (served from 1871 to 1876).

In 1877, federal troops were withdrawn from Florida as the Radical Reconstruction era ended. With no federal oversight, White Florida legislators used poll taxes, literacy tests, Jim Crow laws and intimidation to control Black citizens. Florida's state political system was completely returned to White dominance. Most of the rights Black citizens gained during the Reconstruction era quickly eroded in Florida.

CHAPTER 16

JIM CROW AND THE MODERN CIVIL RIGHTS ERA

RACIAL SEGREGATION DEFINED

Racial segregation is the legal practice of separating people into racial or other ethnic groups. The practice usually restricts specific groups of people to distinct residential areas. It also mandatorily restricts specific groups of people in the use of societal institutions, including churches, hospitals, theaters and schools, and public facilities such as parks, playgrounds, restrooms and waiting areas. Eating in restaurants, staying in hotels, riding buses, drinking from water fountains, visiting medical doctors' and dentists' offices and attending movies are segregated by specific groups of people. Racial segregation gives a politically dominant group the legal authority to maintain social, economic and educational advantages over other groups of people, regardless of the demographics of an area.

After the end of Reconstruction in 1877, Florida, as well as all other states in the Deep South, adopted the concept of Jim Crow (legal racial segregation with the delusion of "separate but equal").

The Jim Crow era lasted from 1877 to 1968 and created a historic racial divide in Florida and most other parts of the United States. The dominant racial group in Florida, and the United States, during the Jim Crow era was Whites, who benefited economically, educationally and societally from the legal oppression of Black people and other people of color. The U.S. military remained racially segregated until after World War II ended. It took the prowess of President Harry S. Truman to issue Executive Order 9981 in 1948, which mandated the desegregation of all U.S. military forces.

PROPAGANDA DURING THE JIM CROW ERA

PROPAGANDA DEFINED

Propaganda is defined by Britannica as "the more or less systematic effort to manipulate other people's beliefs, attitudes, or actions by means of symbols (words, gestures, banners, monuments, music, clothing, insignia, hairstyles, designs on coins and postage stamps, and so forth)." Oftentimes propaganda includes lies and misinformation, and it can also censor facts in an attempt to sway public opinion.

Propaganda associated with racial segregation during the Jim Crow era

typically portrayed Blacks as buffoons, cannibalistic, obedient servants, menaces to society, pitiable exotics, and self-loathing victims with the intention to demean the entire race of people. Dehumanizing and anti-Black depictions were displayed in a vast array of everyday stereotypical material objects such as tourist souvenirs, posters, kitchen utensils, figurines, food containers, fishing lures, advertisements, signs, television shows, toys, movies (including some Disney productions), postcards and cartoon-type caricatures.

Much of the propaganda associated with racial segregation during the Jim Crow era concentrated on the Deep South; however, some targeted northern and western states as well. Such propaganda specific to Florida was plentiful, and some of it was intentionally demeaning toward Black people. Some of this propaganda actually lured tourists from the north to Florida using racist and dehumanizing images of Black people. Florida's rural and agricultural settings, where many Black people were employed as sharecroppers and in other manual labor jobs, were common themes. Alligators (Florida's most famous wild predator) were often graphically depicted stalking and attacking Black children, who were viciously referred to as "alligator bait."

WATERMELON JIM, FLORIDA

Ah don't bother work; work don't bother me;
Ah'm just as happy as a bumble bee,
Ah eats when I can get it, watermelon 'm fine,
'N dis nigger never leaves de rhine.

Left: Watermelon Jim, Florida. This circa 1925 postcard includes a racist poem: "Ah don't bother work; work don't bother me; / Ah'm just as happy as a bumble bee, / Ah eats when I can get it, watermelon 'm fine, / 'N dis nigger never leaves de rhine." Note the handwritten correspondence at the top: "Haven't seen any watermelon yet but Negroes, Oh! My!" *Author's collection.*

Below: Hand fan, circa 1920s, from the Saint Petersburg Alligator Farm. One side reads "Alligator Bait"; on the other, "State of Florida" and "Land of Gators." *Author's collection.*

RACIAL TERROR AND LYNCHINGS IN FLORIDA

In 1900, the population of Florida was only 528,542 (44 percent were Black). Until the mid-twentieth century, Florida was the least populated state in the Deep South. During the twentieth century, Florida experienced some horrific acts of racial terror and violence against Black people, including the Ocoee Massacre (called the "single bloodiest day in modern American political history," when a White mob attacked and killed 30 to 80 Black citizens who wished to vote), the Perry Race Riot (a racially motivated riot in which a group of Whites killed four Black men—one was lynched and burned at the stake—after a White female schoolteacher was murdered) and the Rosewood Massacre (a race riot in which nearly the entire town of Rosewood was destroyed and at least 6 Blacks and 2 Whites were killed; some estimates indicate that 27 to 150 Blacks were killed).

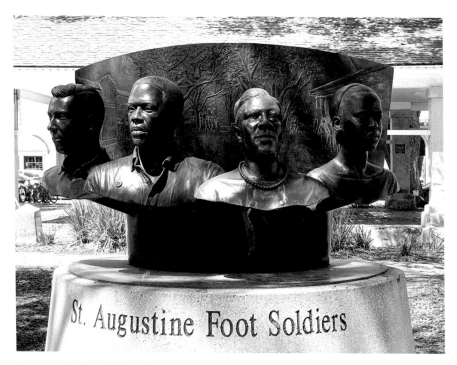

St. Augustine Foot Soldiers Monument, located near the Plaza de la Constitución and dedicated to the people who protested peacefully in the early 1960s to advance the civil rights cause in St. Augustine and elsewhere. It was installed and unveiled in May 2011. *Courtesy of Wikimedia Commons.*

THE ORIGIN OF THE NAME JIM CROW

The origin of the name Jim Crow dates to the 1830s, when a White actor named Thomas Dartmouth "Daddy" Rice is said to have heard an elderly Black man singing the song "Jump Jim Crow." Daddy Rice then created minstrel routines using the fictional name Jim Crow in which he acted the part of an awkward simpleton Black slave and achieved national and international fame in doing so.

Between 1865 and 1950, Florida led the nation in the number of racial terror lynchings per capita. At least 350 lynchings occurred in Florida during this time; however, the accurate total number may never be known as many terror attacks were not publicly documented. These lynchings were extrajudicial public demonstrations used to instill fear in entire Black communities and to maintain White-dominated social control.

THE MODERN CIVIL RIGHTS MOVEMENT (1948–68)

The modern Civil Rights Movement was successful at breaking down many racial barriers and responsible for the national outlawing of Jim Crow laws.

Following the conclusion of World War II, massive numbers of U.S. citizens grew discontented with racial segregation. After all, the United States and its allies had just defeated the authoritarian and totalitarian governments of the Axis powers, and yet the United States still allowed legalized racial segregation in many of its states, including Florida.

Florida played an important and instrumental role in the modern Civil Rights Movement. Many significant boycotts, protests, riots and sit-ins occurred within its borders, including the Tallahassee Bus Boycott (1956). In Tallahassee, as well as many other cities with segregated busing, the rules for riders were as follows: White riders sat in the front and Black riders in the back. If there were no vacant seats in the back, Blacks had to stand (even if there were vacant seats in the front); if there were no vacant seats in the front, Blacks had to relinquish their seats to Whites.

On May 26, 1956, two Florida A&M University students, Wilhelmina Jakes and Carrie Patterson, were arrested and charged with "placing themselves in a position to incite a riot." They were attempting to terminate racial segregation on Tallahassee's buses. A citywide bus boycott was launched. Negotiations between the NAACP and local Black community leaders and the City of Tallahassee ended the boycott on December 22, 1956. The Tallahassee city commission ended official racial segregation on buses on January 7, 1957, due to the ruling in the case of *Browder v. Gayle*. The U.S. Supreme Court upheld a June 5, 1956 district court ruling that stated, "The enforced segregation of Black and White passengers on motor buses...violates the Constitution and laws of the United States." The ruling was based on peoples' rights of equal protection under the Fourteenth Amendment of the U.S. Constitution.

Jacksonville's Ax Handle Saturday (1960): A group of approximately two hundred White men, some suspected of being Ku Klux Klan members, used baseball bats and axe handles to attack Black people who were engaged in peaceful sit-ins at Whites-only lunch counters in the Woolworth's and W.J. Grant department stores, protesting racial segregation. The police did not make any arrests during the violence until a Black street gang named the Boomerangs showed up to protect the protestors. Many of the Boomerang members and other Black residents were arrested. Politicians, including Jacksonville's mayor Haydon Burns, and the local media attempted to downplay the violence. However, *Life* magazine and many newspapers outside of Jacksonville covered the story, which exposed Jacksonville's segregation problems. Jacksonville's Ax Handle Saturday incident led to the desegregation of the city's lunch counters in 1961.

The St. Augustine Movement (1963–64): A localized Florida part of the national modern Civil Rights Movement. As the city of St. Augustine was

On June 18, 1964, hotel manager and segregationist James Brock deliberately poured muriatic acid (a highly corrosive and toxic chemical compound) into the pool of the Monson Motor Lodge in St. Augustine while Black and White protesters were swimming. *Courtesy of Wikimedia Commons.*

EXAMPLES OF JIM CROW LAWS IN FLORIDA

1885: The Fifth Florida Constitution (Article XII, Section 12) stated: "White and Colored children shall not be taught in the same school, but impartial provision shall be made for both." Also, Article XVI, Section 24 stated: "All marriages between a White person and a Negro, or between a White person and a person of Negro descent to the fourth generation, inclusive, are hereby forever prohibited."

1903: A Florida statute made intermarriage with a "Negro," "Mulatto" or any person with one-eighth Negro blood illegal. Penalty: imprisonment up to ten years or a fine not more than $1,000.

1913: A Florida statute made it unlawful for White teachers to teach Negroes in Negro schools and for Negro teachers to teach in White schools. Penalty: Violators subject to fines up to $500 or imprisonment up to six months.

preparing for its four hundredth anniversary celebration, a high-profile event of national importance, its racial segregation battles significantly overshadowed its celebration as the oldest continuously occupied settlement of European and African American origin in the United States.

Martin Luther King Jr. traveled to St. Augustine in 1964 to put a spark into the modern Civil Rights Movement. He spoke at churches, appeared at organized demonstrations in the city's Plaza de la Constitución and met with local civil rights leaders. He had to stay at different houses as a safety precaution as his life was threatened several times. On June 5, 1964, King announced at a news conference that St. Augustine was the most lawless community he had encountered.

On June 11, 1964, King was arrested on the doorstep of the Monson Motor Lodge for trespassing and violating Florida's unwanted guest law. The Monson Motor Lodge had a Whites-only policy. King spent the night in the St. Johns County Jail. This incident, as well as beatings, attacks and arrests of nonviolent civil rights activists in St. Augustine, made national headlines.

On June 18, 1964, seventeen rabbis were arrested at the Monson Motor Lodge for "assembling in an integrated group as a protest against racial segregation, discrimination and violence." This remains the largest group arrest of rabbis in U.S. history. On the same day, several demonstrators, Black and White, jumped into the Monson Motor Lodge's swimming pool. The lodge forbid Black people to swim in its pool due to racial segregation laws. In an act of cruelty, James Brock, the manager of the lodge, poured muriatic acid into the water. (Exposure to muriatic acid can cause numerous health problems, including severe skin burns, irreversible eye damage or blindness and lung and nose lining damage if it is inhaled.)

Photographs of the Monson Motor Lodge incident, coupled with those of a police officer jumping into the pool to arrest the demonstrators, made headlines around the country and the world. These photographs are now some of the most famous images of the modern Civil Rights Movement. People around the country and the world voiced outrage at the brutality against civil rights demonstrators in St. Augustine. This incident had a huge influence on many members of the U.S. Congress as they prepared to vote on pending civil rights legislation.

On July 2, 1964, President Lyndon B. Johnson signed the landmark Civil Rights Act of 1964, which prohibits discrimination on the basis of race, color, religion, sex or national origin.

CHAPTER 17

HENRY MORRISON FLAGLER

In 1883, industrialist and financier Henry Flagler arrived in Florida for the first time, pursuing a warmer climate for his ill wife. He perceived Florida as a backward wilderness that had the potential to be a business, residential and vacation center. In 1885, he began building the elegant Ponce de Leon Hotel in St. Augustine. He quickly realized that Florida's railway systems were inefficient for both freight and passenger service, so he started to purchase railroad companies with the idea of connecting the east coast of Florida with fast and proficient transportation service and routes. His Overseas Railroad project, also called Flagler's Folly, connected the Florida peninsula to Key West, a distance of 128 miles. It was started in 1905 and completed in 1912. This transportation project is considered an engineering marvel and is popularly known as the "Eighth Wonder of the World." Flagler was also instrumental in the development and expansion of several cities, including Miami and Palm Beach. Flagler is credited as the most important player in the modernization of Florida's east coast.

RAILROAD AND TRANSPORTATION MODERNIZATION

In 1885, Flagler purchased the Jacksonville, St. Augustine and Halifax River Railway, which provided railroad service from Jacksonville to St. Augustine.

In 1888, Flagler purchased three other railways: the St. Johns Railway; the Jacksonville, St. Augustine and Halifax River Railway; and the St. Augustine and Palatka Railway. These railways expanded his network from Jacksonville southward through Palatka to Ormond and Daytona.

In 1892, Flagler created a holding company for his growing railway network called the Jacksonville, St. Augustine and Indian River Railway Company. A significant problem Flagler had to overcome in the beginning years of his pioneering railroad projects was the different gauge systems early Florida railway systems were using. Many Florida railways could not connect with one another or run on the same tracks. Flagler converted all his railways to standard gauge.

In 1892, Flagler made plans to expand south of Daytona. He used new Florida land grant laws to purchase land to build new railroad tracks (eventually acquiring more than two million acres). On January 29, 1894, Flagler's railroads reached Fort Pierce, and by March 22, 1894, West Palm Beach was connected to Flagler's railway system.

Due to severe freezing weather in Central Florida during 1894 and 1895, Flagler decided to expand his railway system southward to Miami.

On September 7, 1895, Flagler changed the name of his railway system to the Florida East Coast Railway Company, which is still in business today.

On March 3, 1896, Flagler's Florida East Coast Railway Company reached Fort Lauderdale. On April 15, 1896, the railway reached Biscayne Bay (the present-day Miami area, which only had about fifty residents at the time). Flagler famously refused to have the area named after him; instead, he asked residents to name it Miami, which was derived from Mayaimi (the historic name of Lake Okeechobee and the Indigenous people who lived in the surrounding area).

During 1903 and 1904, Flagler extended his railway south of Miami to Cutler Ridge and Homestead, which increased agricultural business in the south Florida area.

Flagler's railway system generated revenue for many Florida towns along its routes and spurred infrastructure improvements such as electricity, water plants, bridges and roads. Newspapers were also founded in communities along the railway system.

"FLAGLER'S FOLLY"

Arguably, Flagler's greatest achievement was his Florida East Coast Railway's Key West Extension (Overseas Railroad), an engineering project considered so preposterous at the time that it earned the title Flagler's Folly. It was

Henry Flagler arriving on the first Florida East Coast Railway's train to Key West, circa 1912. *Courtesy of Wikimedia Commons.*

inspired by the United States government's 1905 announcement of plans to build the Panama Canal, which Flagler believed would bring profitable shipping business from around the world into Key West. The Overseas Railroad project started in 1905 and took seven years to complete. It cost $50 million ($1.6 billion in 2025 dollars), required thousands of laborers and withstood devastating damage by three major hurricanes. It required innovative engineering designs, including building reinforced-concrete spandrel arches in the open ocean. Dozens of bridges were required, including the Seven Mile Bridge, which featured a 253-foot-long swing span to allow ships to pass between the Florida Bay and Atlantic Ocean. More than 250 people died while working on the project, 135 during the 1906 Florida Keys hurricane.

In 1912, when the Overseas Railroad project was completed, Flagler was eighty-two years old. He rode in his private Florida East Coast Railway car on the ceremonial first ride from West Palm Beach to Key West. Flagler was welcomed with a superb celebration and said, "Now I can die in peace."

The Overseas Railroad operated for twenty-three years, until the 1935 Labor Day hurricane swept away forty-one miles of railroad track and trestles, washed away many miles of roadbed and swept an entire train into the ocean, leaving only its engine on the track. Florida East Coast Railway officials decided not to rebuild for financial reasons and sold the roadbed and remaining bridges to the State of Florida for $640,000.

An Overseas Highway and Bridge District was formed, which developed the former railroad bed into a roadway. The Overseas Highway formally opened in 1944.

LUXURIOUS HOTELS

Built between 1885 and 1887, the Hotel Ponce de León in St. Augustine was Flagler's first hotel. The structure is a masterpiece of Spanish Renaissance architecture and was the first major poured-in-place concrete building in the United States. Thomas Edison's company installed four thousand electric lights, making it one of the first electrified buildings in the United States. Louis Comfort Tiffany designed some of the building's interior, including beautiful stained glass and mosaics. It survives as the Ponce de León Hall, the centerpiece of Flagler College. It was added to the National Register of Historic Places on May 6, 1975. It was also designated a National Historic Landmark on February 17, 2006.

In 1888, the Hotel Alcazar opened in St. Augustine. It was one of the first multistory structures built with poured concrete in the United States. The architects modeled its façade after a Moorish palace in southern Spain. It included three separate sections: baths, a casino and the hotel. Entertainment and recreational facilities were a key feature and included a large indoor swimming pool, a grand ballroom, a bowling alley, croquet lawns and tennis courts. The Great Depression forced it to close in 1931. Today, the St. Augustine City Hall and the Lightner Museum occupy the structure.

In 1887, Hotel Cordova was built in St. Augustine, in the Moorish Revival and Spanish Baroque Revival styles. Flagler purchased the structure soon after it opened and renamed it the Cordova. In 1932, the hotel closed due to the Great Depression. Starting in 1968, it was used as the St. Johns County courthouse, which occupied the structure for thirty years. In 1999, it was restored and opened as the Casa Monica Hotel.

In 1900, Hotel Continental was built in Jacksonville, next to a train depot. The large hotel boosted a luxurious interior with 250 guest rooms, 56 baths, an impressive parlor and a large dining room. The exterior was a relatively simple architectural design, painted in a colonial yellow color and featuring signature green blinds. Entertainment amenities included a dance pavilion, a fishing pier, a nine-hole golf course, tennis courts and a riding stable. In 1913, the hotel changed its name to the Atlantic Beach Hotel. On September 20, 1919, it was destroyed by a gruesome fire.

In 1887, Hotel Ormond was built in Ormond by John Anderson and Joseph Price. In 1890, the hotel was purchased by Flagler, who made spectacular improvements as he added three new wings, a saltwater pool and elevators and expanded the number of rooms from seventy-five to four hundred. He also built a railroad bridge over the Halifax River, which allowed railroad cars to stop in front of the hotel. By 1905, the Hotel Ormond was known internationally and had become a playground for the rich and famous. At one time, it was the largest wooden structure in the United States, featuring eleven miles of corridors and breezeways. The hotel eventually lost its appeal to wealthy travelers and was repurposed into a retirement hotel. On November 24, 1980, Hotel Ormond was added to the National Register of Historic Places for its architectural significance. In 1986, the City of Ormond Beach ordered the evacuation of the building due to its deteriorating and unsafe condition. During the next six years, several attempts to save, restore or repurpose the building failed. In 1992, the Hotel Ormond structure was demolished.

In 1894, the Royal Poinciana Hotel was built in Palm Beach, Flagler's first hotel in southern Florida. At the hotel's peak, it offered almost 1,100 rooms and employed a seasonal workforce of around 1,400 people. The hotel attracted many winter visitors and new residents to the previously sparsely populated area and prompted the growth and development of both Palm Beach and West Palm Beach. The 1928 Okeechobee hurricane caused widespread damage to the structure, which forced its closure for repairs. In 1930, it reopened, but the hardships of the Great Depression forced it to close again three years later. In 1935, the Royal Poinciana Hotel structure was demolished.

Portrait of Henry Morrison Flagler. *Courtesy of Wikimedia Commons.*

In 1896, Flagler opened his second hotel in Palm Beach, called the Palm Beach Inn. It was not as luxurious as the Royal Poinciana Hotel, but it overlooked the Atlantic Ocean. In 1901, Flagler doubled the size of the hotel and renamed it the Breakers because many guests requested rooms "down by the breakers." In 1903, while undergoing additional expansion, it was destroyed by a catastrophic fire. In 1904, it was rebuilt entirely of wood in the Colonial architectural style and featured 425 rooms. The impressive structure became internationally known and attracted guests including Andrew Carnegie, J.C. Penney, William Randolph Hearst and members of famous families such as the Astors, Rockefellers and Vanderbilts. In 1925, the Breakers was destroyed by another catastrophic fire. It was rebuilt into a world-class hotel, its architectural style inspired by the Villa Medici in Rome. It reopened in 1926 and stands today as a masterpiece of Gilded Age luxury.

In 1897, Flagler opened the large Royal Palm Hotel in Miami, one of the first hotels in the city. It was six stories tall and included a salon on the top floor. The architectural style of the structure was referred to as "Modern Colonial." It included 450 guest rooms (100 included private baths), electric lighting (the city's first), elevators and a swimming pool. The hotel also featured a main dining room, private dining rooms, parlors, a billiards room and other gaming rooms. The 1926 Miami hurricane severely damaged the structure. It became infested with termites and was condemned. In 1930, the Royal Palm Hotel structure was demolished.

BRIEF BIOGRAPHY OF HENRY MORRISON FLAGLER (1830–1913)

Henry M. Flagler was born on January 2, 1830, in Hopewell, New York, and died on May 20, 1913, in West Palm Beach, Florida. Prior to coming to Florida, he was a partner of John D. Rockefeller in Standard Oil, one of the largest and most powerful corporations in the world. In 1911, the U.S. Supreme Court ruled that it be dissolved under the Sherman Antitrust Act because it was a monopoly that was driving the cost of oil unreasonably high. By 1881, Flagler had stepped away from day-to-day activities of Standard Oil but remained secretary, treasurer and vice president until 1908 and a director until 1911. In 1885, he decided to invest in Florida and develop its east coast into a tourist destination. He built a chain of luxury hotels and modernized railroad transportation along the east coast of Florida. He was married three times, to Mary Harkness (who died on May 18, 1881, after being ill for several years), Ida Alice Shourds (his first wife's nurse, who was ruled insane, allowing Flagler to legally divorce her on August 14, 1901) and Mary Lily Kenan (whom Flagler married less than two weeks after his divorce from his second wife). Some see Flagler as a ruthless nineteenth-century robber baron who became a multimillionaire through secret dealings, corruption and engaging in unethical business practices. Others see him as a brilliant visionary who risked a fortune, made decisions against huge odds and was instrumental in the development and growth of Florida's east coast, which catapulted it into becoming the modern business, agricultural, residential and tourist center it is today.

CHAPTER 18

HENRY BRADLEY PLANT

RAILWAYS, STEAMSHIP LINES AND LUXURY HOTELS

After the American Civil War ended, Henry B. Plant, businessman, entrepreneur and investor, realized there were huge business opportunities in the South as much of its infrastructure, especially railroads, needed to be rebuilt and expanded. Plant purchased several railroads and began building rail networks along the southern Atlantic coastal regions and throughout central and western Florida. Plant's Florida railroads connected with lines to northern markets, which expanded business for the state's industries, including citrus, celery, lumber and phosphate.

In 1882, he created the Plant Investment Company, which grew to include fourteen railway companies, 2,100 miles of rail track, nine steamship lines and eight luxury hotels. Plant's clever and successful system of railroads, steamboats and hotels, mostly in the southern United States, was called the Plant System and made him a multimillionaire.

Plant selected Tampa, a small village at the time, as his home port for a new line of steamships that transported passengers and freight to and from Key West and Havana, Cuba. Plant also used Tampa as the end of the line for his South Florida Railroad. Tampa was originally settled as Fort Brooke in 1823; however, its modern beginnings as a business center and tourist destination are attributed to Henry Plant. The modern development of cities such as Auburndale, Plant City, Port Tampa, Sanford and Trilby are also attributed to Plant.

THE TAMPA BAY HOTEL

Plant owned eight luxury hotels along his rail lines and steamship ports in central and west Florida, including the Inn, Port Tampa (built in 1888); Hotel Kissimmee, Kissimmee (built in 1890); Tampa Bay Hotel, Tampa (built in 1891); the Seminole Hotel, Winter Park (built in 1891); Hotel Punta Gorda, Punta Gorda (built in 1894); Ocala House, Ocala (built in 1895); Hotel Belleview, Bellair (built in 1897); and the Fort Myers Hotel, Fort Myers (built in 1898).

The Tampa Bay Hotel was the grandest and most luxurious of them all and is the only one still standing. It was originally designed to accommodate wealthy guests, mainly during the winter months. It opened on February 5, 1891. The 511-room, five-story resort-style hotel was designed in the Moorish Revival architectural style, selected by Plant for its exotic attractiveness. It cost over $3,000,000, stands on four and a half acres and is a quarter of a mile long. Plant collected ornate artifacts, many very expensive, from Europe to decorate the interior of the hotel.

Plant Hall, University of Tampa's central building, once housed the Tampa Bay Hotel, a resort built by Henry B. Plant in 1891. *Courtesy of Wikimedia Commons*.

The Tampa Bay Hotel was the first hotel in Florida to have an elevator and the first to have electric lighting and telephones in all its rooms. The majority of its rooms included private bathrooms and a full-size tub. Other interesting features of the hotel include six minarets (a type of tower typically built into or adjoining mosques), four cupolas (a tall, dome-like structure on the top of a building) and three domes (an architectural element comparable to the hollow upper half of a sphere). The hotel's detailed decorative work was finished in Victorian Gingerbread styling.

Portrait of Henry B. Plant. *Courtesy of Wikimedia Commons.*

The hotel's grounds, encompassing 150 acres, included twenty-one buildings, a bowling alley, a casino, a golf course, an indoor heated swimming pool and a racetrack.

During the Spanish-American War (April 21 to December 10, 1898), the Tampa Bay Hotel became the headquarters for the U.S. military. Generals and officers, including Colonel Theodore Roosevelt, stayed in the hotel. Enlisted men camped on the hotel grounds. The First U.S. Volunteer Cavalry, famously known as the Rough Riders, practiced battle maneuvers on the grounds.

During the hotel's operating years, from 1891 to 1930, it was known for its noteworthy guests, including many celebrities and political figures such as Babe Ruth, Clara Barton and Winston Churchill.

In 1930, the hotel closed due to the hardships of the Great Depression.

On August 2, 1933, the Tampa Bay Junior College moved into the structure; it evolved into the University of Tampa, which still occupies the building under a long-term lease. The southeast wing of the building was reserved for the Tampa Municipal Museum (renamed the Henry B. Plant Museum in 1974).

On December 5, 1972, the structure was added to the National Register of Historic Places for areas of historical significance including architecture, literature and military.

On May 11, 1976, the structure was officially recognized by the U.S. government as a National Historic Landmark.

BRIEF BIOGRAPHY OF HENRY BRADLEY PLANT
(1819–1899)

Henry B. Plant was born into a farming family on October 27, 1819, in Branford, Connecticut. He was raised by his mother, stepfather and grandmother under Puritan values which dictated a strong work ethic. He started his business career as a captain's boy at the New Haven Steamboat Company. In 1842, he married Ellen Elizabeth Blackstone, and they had two children; their son Morton Freeman Plant survived into adulthood. Plant excelled in the shipping business and was hired at the Adam's Express Company's New York office. In 1854, the Plants moved to Georgia, and Henry was promoted to manager of the Adams Express Company's southern division responsible for express transportation. When the American Civil War was about to break out, Plant reorganized the company's southern assets into the Southern Express Company. In 1861, his wife, Ellen, died. After the Civil War ended, Plant invested in railroads, steamship lines and luxury hotels. In 1873, he married Margaret Josephine Loughman. He connected many parts of Florida with standard-gauge railroad lines, which drastically improved transportation, expanded commercial trade and increased tourism. He was responsible for about two thousand miles of railroad tracks across the state of Florida. Plant's network of railroads and steamship lines was branded the Plant System. In 1895, Plant employed 12,639 people across his empire. In 1898, *Success* magazine recognized him as the "King of Florida" for his significant contributions, having dedicated much energy, money and time to the advancement and development of Florida. Plant died on June 23, 1899, in New York City.

CHAPTER 19

THE WINTER SILENT FILM CAPITAL OF THE WORLD

"HOLLYWOOD EAST"

Around 1908, the silent film industry, mostly independent studios, began setting up operations in Jacksonville. These studios moved from New York and New Jersey because of camera and film problems caused by the cold climate during the winter season: film stock would occasionally fog and freeze up, causing timely and costly production delays. The Jacksonville area provided a year-round mild climate suitable for filming, as well as reliable railroad transportation and many scenic locations nearby, some featuring interesting and picturesque architecture.

Some of the biggest stars of the silent film era worked and lodged in Jacksonville, including Ethel and Lionel Barrymore, Oliver Hardy and Rudolph Valentino. Eventually, Jacksonville was home to approximately thirty film studios. One of these was owned by Richard E. Norman, one of the first to produce "race films," which cast Black actors in positive, non-subservient and leading roles. This was very unusual for the time, especially in the Jim Crow–era segregated Deep South. Norman was personally appalled by what he saw as unethical racial inequalities at the time and vowed to make a difference in the filmmaking industry.

Opposite: A circa 1908 portrait of Ethel Barrymore (1879–1959). She was a stage, screen and radio actress regarded as the "First Lady of the American Theater" and an Academy Award winner. *Courtesy of Wikimedia Commons.*

Left: Poster for the 1926 silent film *The Flying Ace*, which featured an "all-colored cast." *Courtesy of Wikimedia Commons.*

In 1926, Norman Studios produced the acclaimed silent film *The Flying Ace*, which featured an all-Black cast. Such race films were mainly shown to Black audiences, virtually an untapped market during the silent film era.

Norman Studios produced silent films in Jacksonville for approximately ten years, but as silent filmmaking became obsolete (starting in 1927 with *The Jazz Singer*, the first feature-length movie with synchronized dialogue), it failed to make the transition to "talkie" films.

In 2021, the Library of Congress's National Film Registry selected *The Flying Ace* for preservation as it was identified as being culturally, historically and aesthetically significant.

Norman's five-building film studio complex survives as the Norman Studios Silent Film Museum in the Old Arlington neighborhood. It is the only surviving studio from Jacksonville's silent filmmaking era.

JACKSONVILLE'S FILMMAKING DOWNFALL

In the early part of the 1900s, Jacksonville was a conservative and segregated Deep South city. Most residents did not approve of risqué film scenes or the fast-paced, glamorous lifestyle the silent filmmaking industry brought to Jacksonville. When one film company staged a mob scene in downtown Jacksonville, it led to an actual rowdy crowd smashing windows and disrupting business. Another filmmaking annoyance for many Jacksonville residents was gunshots and other loud noises on Sundays while they were attending church services.

In 1917, Jacksonville elected John Wellborn Martin as its mayor. Martin also served as Florida's twenty-fourth governor from 1925 to 1929. Martin and his administration began working to chase the filmmaking industry out of Jacksonville.

Throughout the 1920s, Jacksonville's filmmaking studios relocated to the Los Angeles, California area, which had a better climate (less humidity), oceans and mountains, offering more diversity for film production. The citizenry of Los Angeles was also, on the whole, less conservative than those living in Jacksonville, and *Angelenos* welcomed the flamboyant filmmaking industry to California.

Interestingly, the early film industry in the Los Angeles area was not initially located in Hollywood; it settled first in Edendale and the San Fernando Valley. The film industry gradually moved into Hollywood as it offered open, expansive, flat land during the 1920s and '30s.

The filmmaking industry helped Los Angeles evolve into a major U.S. cultural center, and it is now home to the world's largest film industry by revenue.

CHAPTER 20

PIVOTAL HISTORIC INDUSTRIES

Since the beginning of the 2000s, Florida's significant industries have included tourism and hospitality, real estate and development, aviation and aerospace, clean energy, defense and homeland security, financial and professional services, logistics and distribution, manufacturing, medical and life sciences and technology.

Historically, several industries were pivotal in shaping Florida's culture and contributing to its growth, including citrus, phosphate, sugarcane and turpentine.

CITRUS

Since Florida has become one of the world's leading growers of citrus crops (including grapefruit, oranges, tangerines and mandarins), these products, especially oranges, have become synonymous with the state. Interestingly, citrus is not indigenous to Florida. It originated in Asia and was transported to the New World by Christopher Columbus in 1493. The Spanish brought citrus to Florida in the early 1500s.

Most early attempts to grow citrus crops in Florida, notably during the British period (1763–83), had only marginal success: occasional cold weather and bacterial, fungal and viral diseases ruined large percentages of the crops.

During the 1870s, successful commercial growth of citrus crops in Florida boomed and created "orange fever," which brought many people to the

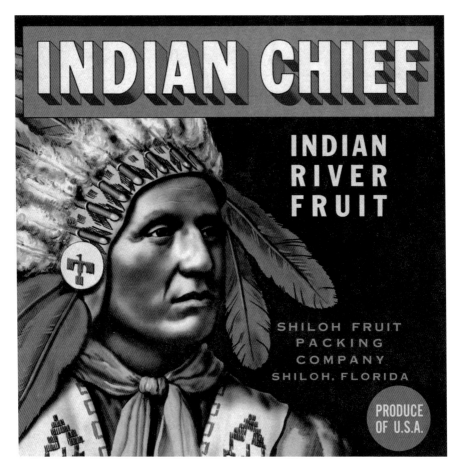

INDIAN CHIEF

INDIAN RIVER FRUIT

SHILOH FRUIT PACKING COMPANY SHILOH, FLORIDA

PRODUCE OF U.S.A.

Historic Florida citrus fruit crate label, Indian Chief brand, from the Shiloh Fruit Packing Company, circa 1940s. *Courtesy of State Archives of Florida.*

state seeking profits. By the 1890s, the citrus industry had created many jobs, especially in northeastern Florida, including for laborers in the groves, factories, packinghouses, steamships and in railroading.

The freezes of 1886 and 1894–95 had a disastrous effect on northeastern Florida, and much of the industry moved farther south. The main areas of Florida's citrus industry became Orange, Lake and Polk Counties.

In 1929, the infestation of the Mediterranean fruit fly halted much of Florida's citrus production. The citrus industry recovered during World War II, when the U.S. government purchased the majority of Florida's crops and the development of frozen concentrate created a year-round source of orange juice.

After World War II, the state's population grew significantly (from 1,897,414 in 1940 to 4,951,560 in 1960), creating demand for housing and community growth. As the cost of doing business in the industry grew and the value of property increased, many family-owned and small citrus growers sold their land. Much of the grove ownership has since shifted to corporations and conglomerates, and Florida's citrus industry is now an agribusiness.

Since 2000, Florida's citrus industry has been dwindling. During the 2000–01 season, Florida produced 78 percent of the citrus in the United States, compared to 17 percent during the 2022–23 season, while California's production has risen to 79 percent of the nation's crops.

As of March 2024, citrus is grown on 332,256 acres (519.15 square miles) in Florida.

PHOSPHATE

Phosphate is a natural, nonrenewable resource that is the natural source of phosphorous, which is widely used for agricultural fertilizer. In the 1880s, phosphate mining began in Florida in the area known as Bone Valley, aptly named for the rich deposits of the fossilized bones of prehistoric animals within its soil. Bone Valley is located mainly in the four counties of Hardee, Hillsborough, Manatee and Polk. Deposits of phosphate in this area account for more than 50 percent of production in the United States.

In the 1890s, the "Great Florida Phosphate Boom" was launched when profitable phosphate deposits were discovered in Marion County and the Peace River area. Hundreds of prospectors flocked into Florida, and by 1894, there were 215 mining operations in business. The boom lasted until 1900. As of this writing, there are twenty-seven phosphate mining operations active in Florida.

Steam shovels became practical after 1900, mechanizing excavation and making picks, shovels and wheelbarrows artifacts of the past. One steam shovel did the work of eighty men and only needed three men to operate it.

Mining phosphate from the ground is one step in processing it. Phosphate must then be separated from the sand and clay that it is mixed with. In the early days of the industry, the separation process was a tedious one, requiring manual washing and screening of the material. In the 1920s, the development of froth flotation tanks automated the separation process. The next industry advancement also came in the 1920s with electric and

A dragline being operated at a phosphate mine field in Bartow, circa 1950s. *Courtesy of State Archives of Florida.*

diesel-powered draglines (heavy-duty excavators). By 1930, draglines had practically replaced steam shovels in phosphate mining. Draglines are still used in the phosphate industry in Florida.

According to information published in 2024 by the Florida Phosphate Council,

> *Approximately 8,400 jobs are directly connected to the phosphate industry in Florida—nearly 50,000 indirectly shaped by its extensive footprint and operational needs. The industry's economic impact in the Tampa region is an estimated $5.03 billion. In fact, well over half of the Port of Tampa's economic activity and jobs are connected to phosphate.*

Phosphate has been good for Florida's economy for more than one hundred years, but the negative side of phosphate mining is the pollution it causes, including "radioactive waste leakage and water pollution that threatens Florida's groundwater resources."

SUGARCANE

Florida is known for its sugarcane production, but this plant is not native to North America as it is indigenous to Asia. In the late 1760s, the British brought it into Florida to be grown on plantations in the northeastern part of what was then the East Florida territory.

In the mid- to late 1800s, due to freezes, Florida's sugarcane industry moved south, seeking warmer weather with more annual rainfall. In the early 1900s, as the Everglades were drained, sugarcane was commercially grown on the farmland the drainage created in areas south of Lake Okeechobee. Despite these commercial operations, a large amount of the sugar coming into Florida was being imported from Cuba.

In 1960, due to the Cuban Revolution, the U.S. government placed an embargo on Cuba that halted the importation of goods, including sugar. The embargo created opportunities for the commercial production of sugarcane in Florida and created "Big Sugar" (the politically powerful industry in Florida). Today, Florida's sugarcane is grown in Palm Beach County (about 70 percent of the acreage) and in Hendry, Glades and Martin Counties (the remaining 30 percent of the acreage).

In 2023, about 17.93 million tons of sugarcane, which equates to about 50 percent of the total value of sugar from sugarcane in the United States, was produced in Florida.

Aerial view of sugarcane fields in the Clewiston region, circa 1980. *Courtesy of State Archives of Florida.*

According to information published in 2024 by the Sugar Cane Growers Cooperative of Florida, "Florida is the nation's largest producer of cane sugar accounting for one in every five teaspoons consumed. The Florida sugar industry has a $2 billion economic impact and generates tens of thousands of jobs."

The sugarcane industry is surely beneficial to Florida's economy, but its negative side effects include sugarcane field burning—an estimated 10,300 fires, which emit over 2,800 tons of hazardous air pollutants every year—and water pollution from field runoff of nutrients like phosphorous, which have had negative environmental affects in the Everglades and other nearby areas.

TURPENTINE

The turpentine industry started in northern Florida in the late 1800s, became a major industry by the early 1900s and existed until the mid-1900s. Turpentine is produced from pine tree sap through a distillation process. Numerous household and commercial products, including cleaners, medicines, paints, soap, shoe polish, varnish and various lubricants, have turpentine as an ingredient. The sticky sap from pine trees was also used as a sealant for wooden ships, and naval stores became a familiar term for the products produced by the turpentine industry.

As large companies purchased timberland or the rights to utilize it, they hired many workers to harvest and distill pine sap from the virgin forests of

Black prisoners caught up in the convict labor system of the state of Florida, circa 1915. *Courtesy of Library of Congress.*

FLORIDA ABOLISHES CONVICT LEASING

On December 31, 1919, the State of Florida abolished its convict leasing (forced labor) program at state prisons. However, county prisons continued to lease convicts to private interests. In 1922, Martin Tabert, a White man from North Dakota who was arrested in Tallahassee on a charge of vagrancy for being on a train without a ticket, was worked to exhaustion and brutally beaten by turpentine camp overseers in front of many witnesses. Laid on a cot and not treated by the camp's medical doctor, he soon died. A public outcry prompted the State of Florida to conduct a high-profile investigation, which revealed corruption, cover-ups and horrific, inhumane treatment of forced labor convicts in turpentine camps. On May 24, 1923, Florida Governor Cary A. Hardee signed the Convict Anti-Whipping Bill, which banned corporal punishment. Florida abolished county convict leasing programs the following day.

---

northern Florida. In 1910, Florida became the top producer of turpentine in the United States.

Work in the turpentine industry was difficult and labor-intensive, and working at the still was a hot and very dirty task. Turpentine companies were notorious for paying low wages, and most used company scrip (non–government issued currency that could only be exchanged in company stores owned by the turpentine companies, which practically ensured employees could not leave as they never made enough genuine money to move elsewhere). In 1938, the Fair Labor Standards Act made payment in scrip illegal in the United States. Most turpentine workers were Black; many were forced to labor under convict leasing programs, in which prisons leased convicts to private companies. Many of these companies did not provide adequate food, water or shelter, and their managers were known to beat and severely punish convicts without judicial or correctional system oversight.

In the early 1940s, the industry began to decline when synthetic methods were developed for the production of turpentine.

By the 1950s, the manual process of traditional turpentine operations was rendered obsolete by newer mechanized processing methods, which were more economical.

By 1970, Florida's turpentine industry had practically disappeared.

CHAPTER 21

FLORIDA DURING WORLD WAR I

The shifting balance of power and economic competition between the coalitions of the Central Powers or Central Empires (principal powers: Austria-Hungary, Bulgaria, Germany and the Ottoman Empire) and the Allies (principal powers: the Empire of Japan, France, the Kingdom of Italy, the United Kingdom, the Russian Empire and the United States) created global tensions during the nineteenth century and into the twentieth century.

On June 14, 1914, a Bosnian Serb student assassinated Archduke Franz Ferdinand, heir to the throne of Austria-Hungary. This incident led to Austria-Hungary declaring war, by telegram, with Serbia on July 28, 1914, igniting World War I.

World War I was one of the deadliest military conflicts in world history, known for combatants' use of chemical (gas) weapons, heavy artillery, machine guns and trench warfare.

The United States was hesitant to enter World War I, and on August 4, 1914, President Woodrow Wilson declared that the United States would remain neutral. However, the United States continued to trade and loan money to certain warring nations, notably favoring France and the United Kingdom over Germany.

Germany's submarine fleet continued to attack passenger and merchant ships, including the sinking of the British ocean liner RMS *Lusitania*, which killed 128 U.S. citizens. Germany's actions against nonmilitary targets swayed public opinion, and on April 6, 1917, Congress voted to declare war on Germany, launching the United States into World War I. Between 1917

"House Passes War Resolution; U.S. in War." *From the* Tampa Morning Tribune, *April 6, 1917.*

and 1918, over four million men and women from around the nation served in the U.S. armed services; 2.8 million men were drafted under the Selective Service Act.

FLORIDA'S ROLE

When the United States entered World War I, Florida had only 925,641 inhabitants; however, 42,030 served in the military.

During World War I, Florida had plenty of open land that was undeveloped and arable. The state's year-round mild climate attracted the military forces to build bases, airfields and training centers.

The director of the U.S. Food Administration, Herbert Hoover, stated that "food will win the war." Florida Governor Sidney Catts responded by encouraging Florida's farmers to produce greater amounts of food and conserve food and crucial products, including meat, sugar, oil, soap and gas. Governor Catts proclaimed May 6, 1917, "National Crisis Day." Farmers in Florida responded by producing a large amount of food to support the war effort. Agriculture and other food products became Florida's largest contribution to World War I. A national sugar shortage spawned large-scale sugar production in the Florida Everglades.

Renewed patriotism prompted citizens to purchase liberty loans and war savings stamps and to produce and conserve food. Volunteerism also increased, benefitting organizations like the Red Cross.

Thousands of Black people frustrated with Florida's oppressive Jim Crow racial segregation laws fled the state for higher wages and more equitable treatment in northern and western industrial cities where wartime contracts offered a higher standard of living.

Fears of German espionage and anti-German sentiment swept through the United States and led to a heightened hatred and distrust of all things

German. Propaganda led to concert halls banning the music of German composers. High schools banned German language programs. German dog breeds were killed. German-language church services and publications were halted. German-language books were burned. Many German food items were renamed, including frankfurters ("liberty sausage"), hamburgers

Opposite: Flagler County resident Fred Benson Miller in his "doughboy" military uniform. He served in the U.S. Army during World War I and survived the conflict to return to civilian life. *Courtesy of Flagler County Historical Society.*

Above: Lakeland Area Company D troops marching to the railroad station during World War I, photographed on September 16, 1917. *Courtesy of State Archives of Florida.*

("liberty steak") and sauerkraut ("liberty cabbage"). Such anti-German sentiment prompted the Florida legislature to pass a law requiring all "aliens" to register with local police.

On November 11, 1918, Germany and its allies surrendered, ending World War I. Thereafter, veterans of World War I were honored annually on Armistice Day, November 11. In 1954, Armistice Day was changed to Veterans Day throughout the United States, which honors all military veterans.

During World War I, of the 42,030 Floridians that served in the military, 1,134 died. Over 30 percent (13,000) of the troops who served from Florida were Black. This was despite the fact that President Wilson proclaimed, "*The world must be made safe for democracy*" while the U.S. Armed Forces remained racially segregated throughout the war and Jim Crow laws were being legally enforced in Florida and elsewhere around the nation.

CHAPTER 22

THE 1920 OCOEE ELECTION DAY RIOTS

On November 2, 1920, the day of the United States presidential election, an organized mob consisting of Ku Klux Klan members and other White supremacists, numbering approximately one hundred, violently attacked Black residents in Ocoee as a warning to those who registered or attempted to vote. Most of the Black-owned buildings and homes in the northern section of Ocoee were burned and destroyed. Two Whites were killed in an initial gun battle, and it's estimated that six to more than fifty Black people were killed during the duration of the mob attack. Those who did survive abandoned their possessions as they were driven out by threats of continual violence, and Ocoee became a virtual sundown town (excluding non-Whites during nighttime hours) for more than fifty years.

Since Ocoee is close to Orlando, the story leaked out and was covered by the local *Orlando Sentinel* newspaper and then published in many newspapers throughout Florida, the nation and internationally, including the *Miami Herald*, the *Buffalo Times* (New York), the *Lancaster New Era* (Pennsylvania), the *Grand Forks Herald* (North Dakota), the *New York Times* and the *Border Cities Star* (Windsor, Ontario, Canada). Although this Ocoee incident received more news coverage than most other similar contemporary race-related atrocities, a local cover-up of the facts, continued threats of more violence and a lack of witnesses willing to testify prevented anyone from ever being convicted of these crimes. The 1920 Ocoee Election Day Riots (also known as the Ocoee Massacre) was one of the nation's ugliest episodes of racial terror, and November 2, 1920, has been referred to as the "single bloodiest day in modern American political history."

EVENTS LEADING TO THE OCOEE MASSACRE

When the American Civil War ended in 1865, so did the institution of slavery, and all Black people in the United States became legally free. Among the implied civil rights were the rights of citizenship, including access to education, improved employment opportunities and the right to vote. The passage of three new amendments to the United States Constitution—the Thirteenth Amendment, (1865), which abolished slavery and involuntary servitude; the Fourteenth Amendment (1868), which prohibited the deprivation of "life, liberty, or property without due process of law" and the Fifteenth Amendment (1870), which prohibited denying any citizen the right to vote based on "race, color or previous condition of servitude"—seemed to have solidified new rights for all Black people. However, the reality of equality and true freedom for Black citizens would take many more decades to achieve.

In 1877, after the Reconstruction era ended, the Democratic Party (which was the party of racial segregation during this time) took back control of all former Confederate states and began passing Jim Crow racial segregation laws, which effectively relegated Black people to the status of second-class citizens. The disenfranchising of Black men (women did not gain the right to vote in the United States until 1920) was accomplished through legal maneuvering that included poll taxes (voting fees), literacy tests (which were arbitrarily conducted by White test administrators who frequently, if not always, failed Blacks) and Whites-only Democratic Party primary elections.

During World War I, approximately 380,000 Black Americans served in the United States military (in racially segregated units). When the war ended in 1918, Black veterans returned home expecting to be rewarded for serving their country and defending democracy. However, there was a resurgence of the Ku Klux Klan, racial violence, hostility, discrimination and lynchings (at least 11 Black World War I veterans were lynched before the end of 1919).

Black people fought back with various organizing campaigns and by establishing legal organizations like the National Association for the Advancement of Colored People (formed in 1909) in an attempt to defeat White supremacy. The Black working-class movement in Florida formed labor unions whose members had to register to vote or be expelled. Supporters of the women's suffrage movement (the struggle for the right of all women to vote in elections) allied themselves with the Florida voter registration movement and successfully encouraged many Black men and women to register to vote in record numbers in the 1920 presidential election.

This progress by Black people caught the attention of White political and community elites and the Ku Klux Klan, who feared that if Black citizens voted in large numbers, they would put an end to racial segregation and end the South's one-party racist rule. In the days leading up to the 1920 presidential election, the Ku Klux Klan marched through the streets of many Florida towns, including Daytona, Orlando and Tampa, in full regalia, spreading threats of violence and warning that "not a single Negro will be permitted to vote."

UPROAR AT THE POLLING PLACE

On November 2, 1920, Election Day, Black citizens entered the polling place in Ocoee despite the resistance of the White community. When they attempted to vote, White poll workers challenged their eligibility and instructed them to prove they were legally registered by appearing before a notary public named R.C. Bigelow, who was absent from his office as he was on a fishing trip for the day and could not be contacted. Several Black people were outraged, including Mose Norman, a prosperous farmer and an organizer of the local voter registration drive, and he attempted to vote despite being rejected by the White poll workers, who then claimed he failed to pay his poll tax and disallowed him from voting. Norman and other Black people were then pushed and shoved away from the polling place without being given the opportunity to vote.

Determined to vote, Norman contacted Judge Moses Cheney. Cheney, a Republican, supported Black voter registration drives and had also been threatened by the Ku Klux Klan, for legal advice he had given to Blacks. Judge Cheney told Norman that obstruction of voting is illegal and advised him to record the names of the Black people who were denied the right to vote and the names of the Whites who were violating their constitutional rights. Norman was so upset at the injustice that he returned to the polling place with a shotgun in his car along with several dozen friends and neighbors, demanded the poll workers' names and shouted, "We will vote, by God!"

Members of the Ku Klux Klan were watching over the polling place, and when they discovered a shotgun in Norman's car, they pistol-whipped him and chased him away. Many local Whites were marching up and down the streets near polling places and were successful at intimidating and chasing away other Blacks who were trying to vote. As a result, most of the Black registered voters in Ocoee were not able vote in this election.

THE MOB ATTACK

That night, a paramilitary mob of about one hundred Whites, many of them suspected Ku Klux Klan members, led by Colonel Sam Salisbury, the former chief of police of Orlando, searched Ocoee for Norman with intentions of punishing him for attempting to vote and challenging the poll workers' unsanctioned authority. They were informed that Norman was at the house of another Black man named Julius "July" Perry, a deacon in his church, local labor leader, businessman and landowner who was instrumental in registering many Black people to vote.

The mob surrounded Perry's house and demanded that Norman and Perry surrender. When they realized that the men inside were going to stand their ground, they attempted to kick in the front door. Gunshots rang out from inside of Perry's house as the Black men attempted to defend themselves. Colonel Salisbury forced the back door of Perry's house open and was shot in the arm. A gun battle ensued. July Perry was shot and wounded inside his house, and two White men from the mob, Elmer McDaniels of Ocoee and Leo Borgard of Winter Park, were shot and killed in the melee. The White mob retreated and sent for reinforcements from Orlando and other nearby towns.

Perry fled from his house, with assistance from his wife, into a nearby cane field. However, the White mob captured Perry and placed him under arrest. He was treated at the Orlando General Hospital for his gunshot wound and then taken to a jail in Orlando.

Meanwhile, other Whites from the mob torched the entire Ocoee Black neighborhood called the Methodist Quarters. They burned down twenty-five houses, two churches and a fraternal lodge. As Black people fled the burning buildings, snipers from the mob fired at them, killing an undetermined number, including a pregnant woman. All the Black residents who were not killed fled Ocoee and settled in other towns. The exiling of the surviving Black residents and witnesses' reluctance to tell their stories contributed to the fact that the accurate number of Black people killed in the melee has never been established.

Black victims of the Ocoee Massacre included Langmaid, a carpenter who was beaten and castrated; Maggie Genlack and her pregnant daughter, who died while hiding in a burning home; and Roosevelt Barton, who hid in Perry's barn and was shot while fleeing after the mob set the structure ablaze.

One example of a contemporary southern White newspaper's account of the Ocoee Massacre is a November 4, 1920 *Miami Herald* front-page article that states:

> *Number of dead in Ocoee not known—town and nearby swamps patrolled by armed citizens following cold-blooded killing of two young White men and lynching bee* [a hanging] *of their slayer—"Bad" Negro went to the polls with gun—five cremated when fire sweeps Black belt; explosions in burning houses indicate Negroes had plentiful supply of rifles and ammunition.*

THE LYNCHING OF JULIUS "JULY" PERRY

A short time after July Perry was jailed in Orlando, a White mob reportedly overwhelmed the jailer and dragged Perry from his jail cell. The mob brought Perry's beaten, bullet-riddled body to the corner of Colonial Drive and Orange Blossom Trail in Orlando, where they lynched him from a light post. A frightening and intimidating note was posted near Perry's body: "This is what we do to niggers who try to vote."

The morning of November 3, 1920, Perry's body was reportedly cut down by Orange County Sheriff John Frank Gordon, and he was pronounced dead by the coroner. A Black undertaker named Edward Stone buried Perry in an unmarked grave in the Black section of Orlando's Greenwood Cemetery. It was not until 2002 that Perry's grave site was identified with a headstone.

It was reported that a local photographer sold pictures of Perry's body for twenty-five cents each and that several local stores placed these photos in their window displays as instruments of power and intimidation.

Perry's wife and daughter survived the Ocoee Massacre, and local authorities sent them to Tampa for medical treatment and "to avoid further disturbance." They never returned to Ocoee.

Photograph of Julius "July" Perry, circa 1915. *Courtesy of Smithsonian Open Access Initiative.*

132

EXODUS OF BLACK PEOPLE FROM OCOEE

Following the Ocoee Massacre, the Black survivors who hid in nearby swamps, woods and orange groves were driven out of town by threats of more violence and the loss of their residences. Black citizens of the southern part of Ocoee called the Baptist Quarters, who were not targeted by the initial mob attack, were physically threatened into abandoning their property and homes as well. Many fled to the neighboring towns of Winter Garden and Apopka, which had fairly large Black populations in 1920. Approximately five hundred Black residents were driven out of Ocoee, leaving the town predominately populated by Whites.

MORE THAN A CENTURY LATER, FLORIDA AND THE NATION REMEMBER

The Ocoee Massacre targeted Black peoples' economic success and progress toward racial equality and oppressed their right to vote. White supremacists and the Ku Klux Klan organized a paramilitary operation that used intelligence gathering to threaten, beat and murder Black leaders and innocent citizens and destroy their property. The mob attack in Ocoee effectively prevented Black people from voting and from challenging the White-dominated political structure in the area. No one was ever convicted of these horrific crimes, and as they began to fade from memory, they were almost forgotten. However, recent efforts by activists and media outlets, including a documentary film titled *Go Ahead On, Ocoee* (2002) and a documentary broadcast in 2020 by Orlando's WFTV 9 (ABC), propelled the story into the mainstream and ensured it will be taught in Florida public schools. Additionally, many communities, including Orlando and Ocoee, have pledged to take responsibility for remembering their past, including its atrocities, and to respect diversity to ensure such ghastly events never occur again.

CHAPTER 23

THE FLORIDA LAND BOOM AND BUST OF THE 1920s

The Florida land boom of the 1920s began in the Miami area. It was strategized by Carl Graham Fisher, a pioneer in the automobile industry and a highway construction and real estate developer. Fisher launched a clever nationwide advertising campaign that promoted beautiful and potentially profitable Miami Beach real estate. Fisher's advertising strategy managed to change the image of Florida as a rugged "pioneer" state. Suddenly, thousands of people were lured into the state seeking profitable investments and a quality life in a tropical climate.

BRILLIANT MARKETING CAMPAIGNS

Ready-made cities were created by brilliant marketing campaigns, including Coral Gables, Hialeah, Boca Raton and Venice. Hundreds of subdivision communities were built in Florida, many including fancy, alluring and flashy entranceways.

The Florida land boom inspired the Mediterranean Revival architectural style to prosper, blending Gothic, Italian, Mediterranean, Spanish and Venetian details into many structures, including apartment buildings, commercial complexes, luxurious hotels, mansions and smaller residences.

The national media published overblown stories full of accolades for the benefits of living and investing in Florida, including the state's loose adherence to Prohibition (which prevented the manufacture, sale and transportation of alcoholic beverages within the United States and was the law of the land from 1920 to 1933 under the terms of the Eighteenth Amendment). It was

Florida billboard promoting the sale of land lots in Miami, circa 1922. *Courtesy of Wikimedia Commons.*

Built in 1925, the Tarragona Tower in Daytona Beach was designed to serve as a showy entranceway to the thousand-acre Coquina Highlands residential development. *Photograph by author.*

assumed that Florida allowed easy access to beer, wine and spirits, but that was not completely true: local law enforcement and agents from the Bureau of Prohibition made many arrests in the state.

The national media also published alluring stories that suggested the possibility of quick real estate fortunes and boosted year-round agricultural opportunities in Florida. Consumer credit was also made available to many who previously were unable to purchase homes and land as they had little money of their own. Speculation soon caused property prices to rapidly rise as the land boom spread to several areas around Florida.

It was not long before the Florida land boom attracted dishonest people, including the infamous Italian swindler and con artist Charles Ponzi, inspiring them to create criminally speculative schemes that defrauded many investors. Ponzi utilized an unscrupulous and fraudulent scheme now known as the Ponzi scheme: an investment fraud that pays existing investors with funds collected from new ones. Ponzi and other fraudsters also sold mail-order building lots that were in swampland or underwater and unsuitable for development.

THE BOOM GOES BUST

Several factors contributed to the downfall of the Florida land boom of the 1920s. By 1925, negative national press regarding Florida investments coupled with IRS investigations had revealed that land prices were based on the expectation of luring customers and not associated with the actual value of the land. Investors and speculators began to have difficulty finding new buyers and closing sales as the truth about Florida land values became public knowledge.

In October 1925, an embargo permitting shipments of essential commodities only (including food, fuel and perishables) to enter or move within Florida was created due to rail traffic gridlock by the Atlantic Coast Line Railroad, the Florida East Coast Railway and the Seaboard Air Line Railway, the three major railroads within the state. This railroad traffic embargo crippled new building construction and drastically slowed down the Florida land boom.

On January 10, 1926, the *Prinz Valdemar*, a 241-foot steel-hulled schooner, sank in the Miami harbor and blocked shipping access to the harbor. Ships could not transport construction materials directly into southern Florida. This event coupled with the railway embargo crippled the Florida land boom in the Miami area and exposed the exaggerated property price escalations. The newly minted national image of Miami, and Florida, as a tropical paradise was rapidly unraveling. The rapid decline of the Florida land boom was underway.

As the Florida land boom began to collapse, many planned communities (such as Flagler City, an advertised boomtown which was just beginning to be developed along the Dixie Highway in western Flagler County) was abruptly halted. By the middle of 1926, advertisements and articles in the *Flagler Tribune*, the local newspaper covering the story, regarding Flagler City had simply vanished. The concept of Flagler City—and many other potential Florida boomtowns—evaporated faster than it began. In the case of Flagler City, decades after the Florida land boom went bust, only some concrete curbing and yellowed newspaper advertisements remained as faint reminders of the once spectacular concept.

Two major hurricanes struck Florida in the 1920s: the Miami hurricane of 1926 and the Okeechobee hurricane of 1928. These enormous storms caused widespread damage. Many land buyers fled, and many developers went bankrupt.

The final nail in the coffin for the Florida land boom came when the Wall Street crash of 1929 occurred, ushering in the Great Depression. These physical and financial disasters officially ended the Florida land boom of the 1920s.

CHAPTER 24

THE 1928 OKEECHOBEE HURRICANE

During the summer of 1928, heavy rains raised the water level of Lake Okeechobee to three feet above normal, setting the stage for the worst storm in Florida history. On September 26, 1928, a ferocious hurricane (now known as the 1928 Okeechobee hurricane or the San Felipe Segundo hurricane) made landfall on the east coast of Florida at West Palm Beach. Before this hurricane arrived in the United States, it had already killed 1,500 people in the Bahamas, Puerto Rico and the Virgin Islands. By the time it reached the Lake Okeechobee area, the winds were not the biggest problem; it was the raging floodwaters that killed the most people.

The 1928 Lake Okeechobee hurricane killed an estimated 2,500 people in the United States (the National Hurricane Service has suggested the number could be as high as 3,000). Most of the casualties were in Florida, and the majority of them were Black migrant farmworkers. Close to half the population of the western part of Palm Beach County was killed. It is the fourth deadliest hurricane in U.S. history, ranking behind the 1900 Galveston hurricane (which killed at least 8,000 and possibly as many as 12,000 people), the 1899 San Ciriaco hurricane (which was the longest-lived Atlantic hurricane on record and killed at least 3,855 people) and Hurricane Maria (which produced 175-mile-per-hour winds, causing widespread catastrophic damage, and killed 3,059 people, 2,975 of them in Puerto Rico, in 2017).

The 1928 Okeechobee hurricane caused an estimated $27 billion worth of damage (in 2025 dollars) and was one of the major reasons Florida was plunged into a severe economic depression before the Great Depression ravaged the entire nation starting in 1929.

The first communities along the Palm Beach County coastline to experience the wrath of the 1928 Okeechobee hurricane suffered horrendous destruction, from Pompano Beach to Jupiter. Many buildings in West Palm Beach were demolished or severely damaged, the majority of Delray Beach was devastated, railroad cars were derailed and a significant number of buildings were destroyed in Boca Raton.

Unimaginable destruction and loss of life occurred inland in the Lake Okeechobee area. The hurricane caused horrific flooding from the lake, destroying twenty-one miles of earthen walls (almost half of the five-foot-tall dikes that were built to hold back waves caused by summer rains). The estimated fifteen-foot-high storm surge on Lake Okeechobee had the ferocity of a tidal wave, and its rushing floodwaters devastated the small farming communities around the southern shores of the lake. Thousands of migrant farmworkers sought shelter in subpar homes and dilapidated structures, but this proved futile for many, who drowned and were washed away by the intense floodwaters.

The recovery of dead bodies was a difficult, dangerous and sickening task. Government officials assisted by hundreds of volunteers sifted through the devastated areas, finding bodies floating, stuck in mud and scattered among the debris. Many pine boxes were quickly built to move the bodies to drier and higher areas for mass burials. Survivor Frank Stallings lost a grocery

Loading bodies of several victims of the 1928 Okeechobee hurricane into a truck at Belle Glade. *Courtesy of State Archives of Florida.*

store business during the hurricane, but his family survived. Stallings and his father volunteered to recover the victims' dead bodies. Years later, he said, "We were hauling bodies out of the water two and three at a time." Stallings recalled that he recognized many faces in the piles of dead bodies. He was sickened by the sights and stench and found it difficult to eat for many days.

After five days of searching, hundreds of bodies had not been recovered and were rotting away in the heat and humidity. Stallings said, "The Health Department instructed my father to build a fire and destroy the bodies because they were getting too far along."

COMPASSIONLESS MASS GRAVES

The burned remains along with the dead bodies of around 1,600 people were trucked to Port Mayaca. Between Pahokee and Sebring, roadside ditches were dug as makeshift mass graves to unceremoniously bury this group of people.

In West Palm Beach's Woodlawn Cemetery, sixty-nine White people were buried in pine boxes. This was considered a proper burial for White people, in accordance with bigoted Jim Crow racial segregation laws. A memorial for these White victims was erected in the Woodlawn Cemetery in 1928.

In West Palm Beach's Pauper's Cemetery (Twenty-Fifth Street and Tamarind Avenue), 674 Black people and others of unknown races were buried in a twenty-foot mass grave without any memorials or grave markers. Some of the victims were buried at other cemeteries: at least twenty-two at Miami Locks (now Lake Harbor), twenty-eight at Ortona and twenty-two in Sebring. It has long been rumored that hurricane victims are buried at the cemetery at Loxahatchee, but this remains unconfirmed.

Historians have suggested that due to Jim Crow–era racism and fears of disrupting the Florida tourism industry, local officials purposefully did not adequately document the severity of the storm and politicians downplayed and covered up its devastation and the many lives lost. These are among the main reasons that the 1928 Okeechobee hurricane remained largely forgotten by the public until 1991, when the Sankofa Society (a student-led community-based organization guided by Georgia State University's Department of Africana Studies) put together a well-publicized ceremony that shined public light on the tragedy.

SOME RECOGNITION AFTER SEVENTY YEARS

After being owned by several private parties for decades, the Pauper's Cemetery property was purchased by the City of West Palm Beach in December 2000, which prevented it from being bulldozed and developed. The Pauper's Cemetery in West Palm Beach was added to the U.S. National Register of Historic Places on September 12, 2002.

In 2003, on the seventy-fifth anniversary of the 1928 Okeechobee hurricane, the City of West Palm Beach placed an historical marker in the Pauper's Cemetery commemorating the victims.

Memorial to victims of the storm of 1928, "Historic Cemetery & Mass Grave Site," located in the Paupers Cemetery in the city of West Palm Beach, Florida. *Courtesy of Wikimedia Commons.*

CHAPTER 25

THE GREAT DEPRESSION

The Great Depression was the longest and most severe economic downturn in the history of the Western industrialized world. It began on "Black Tuesday," October 29, 1929 (the stock market crash of 1929) and lasted until about 1939 in most countries. It lasted until 1941 in the United States. Prior to the Great Depression, Florida's economy had been in a serious statewide recession since its land boom of the 1920s went bust around 1926, stifling credit and causing bank failures. Florida's economy was also marred by two hurricanes in the 1920s: the great Miami hurricane of 1926, which caused catastrophic damage to the Miami and Gulf Coast areas, and the 1928 Lake Okeechobee hurricane, which killed an estimated 2,500 people in the United States. Another blow to Florida's economy occurred in 1929 when the Mediterranean fruit fly infested and destroyed a large percentage of the state's citrus crops. Citrus production fell from 28 million boxes in the 1928–29 season to 17 million boxes the following season.

The Great Depression also significantly slowed down tourism in Florida from three million to one million visitors per year. The reduced numbers of tourists traveling to Florida added to the state's unemployment numbers, reduced state tax revenues and increased reliance on public relief programs.

At the beginning of the 1930s, emergency public relief funds were being paid to 26 percent of Florida's population. More than one out of every five Florida families were struggling to earn enough money to live.

During the Great Depression, farmlands south of Lake Okeechobee provided agricultural jobs picking vegetables and working in canning

An example of the harsh living conditions endured by some migrant workers and their families during the Great Depression in Belle Glade, circa 1939. *Courtesy of State Archives of Florida.*

factories and packing plants. Thousands of poor, displaced and migrant workers, some bringing their desperate family members along, entered the state seeking employment, even though the jobs were typically low paying and required grueling manual labor. Police and armed guards would sometimes monitor the state's borders in an attempt to limit the entry of migrants.

FDR'S "NEW DEAL" TO THE RESCUE

President Herbert Hoover, who had been in office since 1929, did not fully grasp the seriousness of the Great Depression and refused to fully mobilize the federal government through intervention programs and spending as he thought this would lead the nation toward socialism. Hoover was widely criticized and blamed for worsening the conditions of the Great Depression. During Hoover's presidential reelection bid in 1932, he was thoroughly routed by Franklin D. Roosevelt.

After President Roosevelt took office in 1933, he focused on reinflating the economy by championing a series of financial reforms, public works projects and regulations through executive orders and laws passed by Congress. This was government-regulated economics, called the New Deal, specifically designed to help people throughout the nation who were suffering from the effects of the Great Depression. The New Deal concentrated on the "3 Rs": relief for the unemployed (including the poor), recovery of the nation's economy and reform of the financial system geared toward preventing another economic depression.

The New Deal's federal agencies and programs included the Civil Works Administration (CWA), the Civilian Conservation Corps (CCC), the Farm Security Administration (FSA), the National Industrial Recovery Act 1933 (NIRA), the Social Security Administration (SSA) and the Works Progress Administration (WPA).

WPA PROJECTS IN FLORIDA

The Works Progress Administration (WPA), renamed the Works Projects Administration in 1939, was a work relief program that employed over 8.5 million people around the nation until it was shuttered in 1943.

The WPA was extremely important to Florida's economy during the Great Depression. The WPA built new structures including bridges, highways, parks, playgrounds, public buildings, schools and streets, improving Florida's infrastructure. The agency was also responsible for improving many other structures throughout the state.

Some highly visible WPA projects were completed in Florida, including Orlando Stadium, now the Citrus Bowl Stadium, Orlando (built in 1936 as an 8,900-person venue); Fort Jefferson, Key West (structural renovations and historic restoration were completed between 1935 and 1938); and the Oceanfront Park Complex, Daytona Beach (built between 1936 and 1937).

The Oceanfront Complex was one of the most distinctive WPA projects completed in Florida. The large beachfront park was constructed of coquina rock mined in Florida. Originally, the complex included a bathhouse, concessions, coquina rock–veneered shops, game rooms, small rectangular pavilions, stores, octagonal kiosks and two coquina rock–veneered pedestrian underpasses. The band shell and its seating area, the Edward H. Armstrong Monument and the Coquina Clock Tower and its fountain are the surviving parts of the original complex.

Unique coquina clock tower, band shell and arched walls in the Oceanfront Park Complex, Daytona Beach, built by the WPA in 1936–37. Postcard circa 1960. *Author's collection.*

When the United States entered World War II in December 1941, a bustling war economy sprang into action, ending the Great Depression. Florida became home to many military installations, and demand for the state's agricultural products boomed, resulting in the creation of thousands of jobs. Unemployment was no longer a major problem in Florida and elsewhere around the nation.

CHAPTER 26

THE 1935 LABOR DAY HURRICANE

When the 1935 Labor Day hurricane made landfall near Long Key, Florida, on September 2, 1935, it was the strongest storm ever recorded in U.S. history. It set records at the time as the most intense Atlantic hurricane in terms of barometric pressure (892 millibars), the strongest in terms of one-minute sustained winds (between 186 to 189 miles per hour), and the strongest at landfall in terms of one-minute sustained winds (185 miles per hour). It was the first Category 5 hurricane to make landfall in the United States in recorded history, and it caused at least 485 deaths (the total number of fatalities is unknown as some people were swept away into the Atlantic Ocean or the Gulf of Mexico and were never accounted for).

Initial weather forecasts by the U.S. Weather Bureau (predecessor of the National Weather Service) were inaccurate, predicting the storm would pass through the Florida Straits. In 1935, there was no radar or satellites to track storms. The U.S. Weather Bureau's error prevented early evacuation from the areas the storm actually passed through and contributed to the high death toll.

The upper Florida Keys suffered major damage as the storm's surge, eighteen to twenty feet, flooded low-lying areas. Most buildings and trees were destroyed between the communities of Tavernier and Marathon, and the town of Islamorada was literally leveled. Sections of the Key West Extension of the Florida East Coast Railway suffered significant damage and destruction. Congressional records document that 251 World War I veterans who were part of a federal relief project working on the Key West Extension were killed, most of them drowned.

MAKESHIFT WORK CAMPS FOR WORLD WAR I VETERANS

During 1934–35, the federal government sent at least one thousand jobless World War I veterans to the Florida Keys to work on new roads and bridges on the Key West Extension. The veterans were paid $30 per month ($687 in 2025 dollars) and provided free room and board. Makeshift beachfront work camps were set up around Islamorada that included subpar housing shacks located only a foot or two above sea level.

Florida East Coast Railway's rescue train was swept off the tracks by the 1935 Labor Day hurricane. *Courtesy of Library of Congress.*

As the 1935 Labor Day hurricane approached, a Florida East Coast Railway emergency relief train was sent to evacuate the four hundred or so World War I veterans who were sheltering in work camps at the time. The emergency relief train was running late, and as the hurricane made landfall, it blew all the cars off the track, except for the 160-ton engine, before any of the veterans could be evacuated.

The 1935 Labor Day hurricane obliterated the work camps, and by the time the storm passed, more than half of the four hundred or so World War I veterans were dead. Incredibly, almost half the population between Miami and Key West were killed by this horrific storm.

WHO WAS TO BLAME?

As rescuers sifted through the devastated areas, horrific pictures of catastrophic destruction and many dead bodies shocked the nation. Many bodies of victims of the storm were quickly cremated in funeral pyres (heaps of flammable material used for burning a dead body as part of a funeral rite) in an effort to prevent an outbreak of disease.

Officials and the public were especially outraged by the deaths of so many World War I veterans. People demanded to know who was to blame for stranding so many of them in unsafe work camps as a major hurricane ravaged the area.

The Works Progress Administration (WPA), the federal New Deal work program created in 1935 by President Franklin D. Roosevelt that provided employment for millions of casualties of the Great Depression, launched an investigation. WPA officials hastily concluded that the deaths of the World War I veterans were "an act of God." This investigation was disputed by many people and organizations; however, it was supported by WPA officials.

MEMORIAL FOR THE VICTIMS

On November 14, 1937, the Florida Division of the Federal Art Project unveiled a memorial in Islamorada in recognition of victims (veterans and civilians) of the 1935 Labor Day hurricane.

The unique memorial is carved from native Florida Keys limestone and features an eighteen-foot-tall obelisk carved in the shape of a tidal wave with palms bending easterly in the wind. (Some argue the palms should bend

Bodies of several victims of the 1935 Labor Day hurricane being cremated in funeral pyres at Snake Creek. *Courtesy of State Archives of Florida.*

toward the west as the storm made landfall from the east and traveled west; they refer to the memorial as the "Wrong Way Hurricane Monument.") A crypt in the upper level contains the ashes of more than three hundred victims, which were removed from funeral pyres. The cover of the crypt includes green glazed ceramic tiles, twenty-two feet long, featuring a map of the Florida Keys. A bronze plaque is affixed to the memorial that reads, "Dedicated to the memory of the civilians and the war veterans whose lives were lost in the hurricane of September 2, 1935."

President Franklin D. Roosevelt sent a telegram stating, "The disaster which made desolate the hearts of so many of our people brought a personal sorrow to me because some years ago I knew many residents of the Keys."

CHAPTER 27

WORLD WAR II AND THE FLORIDA U-BOAT WAR

On September 1, 1939, World War II began in Europe when German military forces invaded Poland. The United States did not enter World War II until more than two years later, when the Imperial Japanese Navy Air Service launched a surprise attack on the U.S. naval base at Pearl Harbor, Hawaii Territory, on December 7, 1941.

FLORIDA DURING WORLD WAR II

Florida's economy was stagnant due to the Great Depression when the United States entered World War II. The war effort (society's support of its military forces through a coordinated mobilization of industrial, agricultural and human resources) stimulated Florida's economy as thousands of new jobs were created. Florida's year-round mild climate and available land enticed U.S. military forces to build bases and training facilities in many areas throughout the state.

From 1941 to 1945, more than two hundred military facilities, including major bases such as Camp Blanding (located in the city of Starke) and Camp Gordon Johnston (in the city of Carrabelle) and the large naval air stations at Pensacola and Jacksonville, were built or expanded, requiring 1.2 million acres of land. Shipbuilding was Florida's dominant manufacturing contribution to the war effort and was accomplished in ports including Jacksonville, Panama City, Pensacola and Tampa. Two-thirds of Florida's industrial growth during the war was a result of shipbuilding.

Three U.S. airmen from the Ninety-Eighth Fighter Squadron standing next to a Curtiss P-40 Warhawk fighter-bomber aircraft at the Sarasota Army Air Field, circa 1943. *Courtesy of State Archives of Florida.*

Florida's agricultural industry played a vital role in the war effort. Agricultural products including cotton, vegetables and citrus crops were Florida's main exports as they provided large quantities of food for the war effort. Florida's citrus crop production during the war was the largest in the nation. The vast majority of fruit grown in Florida during the war was purchased by the United States government.

More than 248,000 Floridians served in the U.S. Armed Forces during World War II; 3,540 of them died.

THE FLORIDA U-BOAT WAR

During mid-December 1941, Germany sent five U-boats (submarines) on a mission code-named Paukenschlag (Drumbeat) to attack and sink merchant ships off the East Coast of the United States. It became apparent that the U.S. military was not prepared to defend against such an onslaught, and was ineffective against the well-trained and war-experienced German U-boat fleet. Early in the war, the United States did not have enough airplanes, blimps or ships to defend the East Coast and the Gulf of Mexico against U-boat attacks. There were no coastal blackouts in effect, which made ships highly visible and easy targets for U-boats due to bright coastal lights illuminating their silhouettes. By early 1942, German U-boats had been able to sink twenty-five ships. By July 1942, German U-boats had sunk almost four hundred ships, forty of them off the coast of Florida.

The main targets for U-boats were freighter and tanker ships as their demise severely disrupted the supply chain of products supporting the war effort. The U-boat attacks were very close to land, and some were witnessed by civilians, creating fear and tension among the public.

In April 1942, the *Gulfamerica*, an 8,000-ton tanker ship carrying 101,500 barrels of furnace oil, was sailing north off the coast of Jacksonville Beach. It was not sailing in an evasive zigzag course, which was standard while in a combat zone, making it an easy target for a U-boat attack. A German U-boat, *U-123*, torpedoed the tanker. Many people onshore heard an enormous explosion and saw bright flames shooting into the air. Witnesses also saw the U-boat surfacing—it was close enough for them to read its identifying number, 123—to fire its deck gun at the sinking ship. The *Gulfamerica* sank, and 19 of its crew members died.

The sinking of the *Gulfamerica* so close to the U.S. coast and right in front of shocked civilians prompted both military and civilian action. It was obvious that Germany was successfully disrupting shipping activities and was a potential threat to launch land invasions as well.

In Florida, Governor Spessard Lindsey Holland ordered a blackout of coastal area lights. Some beaches were closed at night, all lights in coastal areas were turned off and all windows were required to be shielded with dark covers if internal lights were being used. Automobiles traveling at night near coastal areas were required to have their headlights shielded with black paint.

U.S. and Allied ships traveling on the Atlantic Ocean joined convoys and were escorted by armed naval patrols. Civil Air Patrol aircraft and private vessels assisted with the search to identify U-boats.

The U.S. Navy ordered and deployed blimps that were used in anti-submarine warfare operations. The blimps, equipped with radar and magnetic anomaly detectors (MADs), proved to be very successful at spotting U-boats.

More than 15,200 coastal watchtowers were built and deployed along the Atlantic, Pacific and Gulf of Mexico coastlines. They were arranged approximately every six miles along the coast and manned by Civil Air Patrol and U.S. Coast Guard Auxiliary personnel. Binoculars were used to spot aircraft and U-boats. If any suspicious aircraft or U-boats were spotted,

One of the few surviving World War II coastal watchtowers. This one is located in Ormond Beach. *Photograph by author.*

the towers communicated their observations by telephone to the area's central command station.

By the end of 1942, U.S. and Allied ship attacks in the Atlantic and the Gulf of Mexico had been drastically reduced as the U.S. Navy and the Coast Guard gained military control of U.S. coastal waters. The German U-boat fleet suffered heavy casualties in the Atlantic and elsewhere due to advancements in technology and convoy tactics.

German WWII U-boat *U-534* dry-docked at Birkenhead Docks, Merseyside, England, circa 1945. *Courtesy of Wikimedia Commons.*

In May 1944, the majority of Florida's watchtowers were abandoned because the threat of German U-boat attacks was no longer a major concern.

By the end of the war, 765 of Germany's 1,154 commissioned U-boats had been lost. Over twenty-eight thousand German submariners were killed. This equated to a 75 percent casualty rate, which ranked as the highest among all German forces during the war.

WORLD WAR II ENDS

By the spring of 1945, the German capital of Berlin was under siege: the Western Allies were approaching from the west, and the Soviet Union's forces were assaulting it from the east. On April 30, 1945, Germany's leader, Adolf Hitler, realized it was only a matter of days or hours before his Nazi regime would crumble, so he committed suicide rather than admit defeat and risk his own capture. Grand-Admiral Karl Dönitz assumed the position of head of state of Nazi Germany. On May 8, 1945, Field-Marshal Wilhelm Keitel represented Germany as he signed the German Instrument of Surrender, the official unconditional surrender to the Allies, which also acknowledged the fall of Nazi Germany. May 8 is now recognized as VE Day, which celebrates the ending of World War II in Europe.

Even after Germany's defeat, World War II was still raging between the Allies and the Empire of Japan. It came to an end after the United States' Manhattan Project managed to build two atomic bombs. One was dropped on Hiroshima and the other on Nagasaki in August 1945. On

September 2, 1945, Japan unconditionally surrendered to the Allies aboard the USS *Missouri*, ending World War II. The war was the deadliest military conflict in world history. It caused 419,400 American deaths and over 60 million deaths worldwide (approximately 3 percent of the world's population at the time).

Florida experienced a post–World War II boom: its population steadily increased and its economy became more diverse as many new industries started up or relocated to the state.

CHAPTER 28

THE EVERGLADES

Located in central and south Florida, the area known as the Everglades consists of subtropical wetlands, lakes and rivers. It originally spanned four thousand square miles. It is home to an extraordinarily wide variety of animals, natural habitats and plants. Due to human development and exploitation beginning in the 1800s, it has been reduced to two million acres. It remains the largest subtropical wilderness in North America. The Everglades has been called "a river of grass flowing imperceptibly from the hinterland into the sea." The earliest known human occupation dates to the Late Archaic period, around 4500 BP (before present). The early Paleo-Indian inhabitants were mobile fisher-hunter-gatherers who lived off rich wild food resources in freshwater marshlands and coastal saltwater areas.

Wildlife in the Everglades includes more than 360 species of birds; several are threatened and endangered, including the Cape Sable seaside sparrow, the red-cockaded woodpecker, the snail kite and the wood stork. The Everglades is known for its many species of wading birds (water birds with long legs), including egrets, herons and roseate spoonbills. Many birds are migratory and can be found in the Everglades during the winter months.

Mammals include the Florida panther (the Everglades' most endangered animal) and water mammals such as the bottlenose dolphin and the endangered West Indian manatee.

Reptiles include perhaps the most well-known animal inhabitant of the Everglades, the American alligator. There are also saltwater crocodiles in the Everglades, which are oftentimes mistaken for alligators. Other reptiles

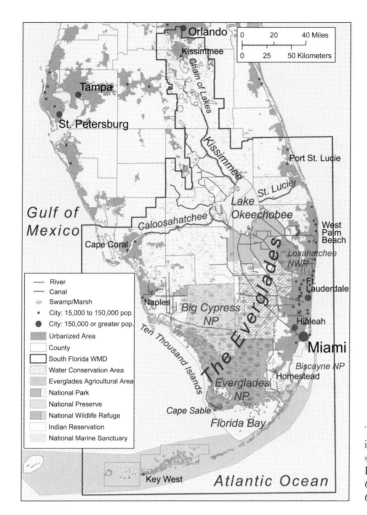

The Everglades is located in the southern third of the Florida Peninsula. *Courtesy of Wikimedia Commons.*

include at least twenty-three species of snakes; four are venomous (the dusky pigmy rattlesnake, the eastern coral snake, the eastern diamondback rattlesnake and the Florida cottonmouth).

The Everglades is home to a variety of plant life, including cypress trees, mangroves, tropical plants and others that are vital to its biological diversity. Plants are the base food supply, providing nutrition and shelter for the animals, birds, fish and insect inhabitants of the entire Everglades ecosystem.

Invasive species are a significant threat to the balance of nature in the Everglades, exploiting and destroying natural resources and outcompeting and killing native species, especially small mammals. Some of the most

Sawgrass prairies are the most prominent feature of the Everglades. *Courtesy of Wikimedia Commons.*

dangerous invasive species include Burmese pythons, feral pigs, lionfish and plants such as the Brazilian peppertree and the Old World climbing fern. Non-native plants have invaded about 1.7 million acres in the Everglades.

DRAINAGE SEVERELY DAMAGED THE ECOSYSTEM

In the centuries before the 1800s, overflowing water from Lake Okeechobee would run through the Everglades and spill into the Florida Bay, which kept nature in balance. Starting in the late 1800s, humans desiring farmland and community development began diverting the natural water flow and building flood control infrastructures, which has drained significant amounts of water and negatively altered the Everglades landscape. This interference with nature has led to a reduction in the size of the Everglades and contributed to adverse effects on the Everglades area. One example of these adverse effects is the degradation of water quality as pollutants from agricultural runoff, roads and buildings has poisoned plant and wildlife.

EVERGLADES NATIONAL PARK

In 1947, the Everglades National Park was established with the support of advocates such as conservationists and scientists. The National Park Service states, "Everglades National Park protects an unparalleled landscape that provides important habitat for numerous rare and endangered species like the manatee, American crocodile, and the elusive Florida panther."

On October 26, 1979, Everglades National Park was designated a World Heritage Site (one of only twenty-five within the United States). World Heritage Sites are designated by the United Nations Educational, Scientific and Cultural Organization (UNESCO), a specialized agency of the United Nations tasked with "the aim of promoting world peace and security through international cooperation in education, arts, sciences and culture."

BRIEF BIOGRAPHY OF MARJORY STONEMAN DOUGLAS (1890–1998)

Portrait of Marjory Stoneman taken during her senior year at Wellesley College, circa 1912. *Courtesy of Wikimedia Commons.*

Marjory Stoneman Douglas was a conservationist, newspaper editor, journalist, women's suffrage advocate and author of the 1947 bestseller *The Everglades: River of Grass*, which shifted public opinion of the Everglades: from an impractical swampy wasteland to a precious and irreplaceable environmental wonderland worthy of preservation. Douglas also founded the Friends of the Everglades, a conservation organization dedicated to protecting the Everglades. Douglas remained active in the preservation and restoration of the Everglades for her entire life; she lived to 108 years of age. The State of Florida named its Department of Natural Resources after her. In 1993, she was awarded the Presidential Medal of Freedom by President Clinton for her lifelong achievements benefiting both the environment and society.

CHAPTER 29

DR. JOHN GORRIE INVENTS AIR CONDITIONING

John Gorrie was born on October 3, 1803, in Saint Kitts and Nevis (West Indies). He was a physician, a scientist and a pioneer in the manufacturing of artificial ice. In 1827, he graduated from the College of Physicians and Surgeons of the Western District of New York in Fairfield, New York. After graduating from medical school, he secured a position as a medical doctor in Abbeville, South Carolina. In 1833, he moved to Apalachicola, Florida, where he continued his career as a medical doctor. He invented an ice-making machine and received a patent for mechanical refrigeration in 1851. Gorrie is considered the father of air-conditioning and refrigeration.

GORRIE'S COOLING SYSTEM

Gorrie began researching tropical diseases while practicing medicine in South Carolina. The hospital where he worked had many patients, mostly seamen, who were suffering from malaria and yellow fever. In 1841, there was an outbreak of yellow fever in Apalachicola, and Gorrie set out on a personal quest to find treatments for the tropical disease.

Gorrie observed that hot and humid conditions made patients' fevers worse and that they were more likely to die due to high fevers. He became convinced that fever caused by tropical diseases could be controlled by constantly circulating cold air in a suffering patient's room. In order to do this, large quantities of ice were required, and at the time, ice in Florida was

Portrait of Dr. John Gorrie, circa 1840s. *Courtesy of State Archives of Florida.*

scarce. Ice had to be harvested from frozen lakes in the north, stored in icehouses and then shipped southward. The supply of ice reaching Florida was unreliable at the time as well. Gorrie decided to invent and build a machine that made artificial ice so it could be readily available.

By 1844, Gorrie had built a working air-cycle refrigeration (artificial ice) machine. After 1845, Gorrie pursued his refrigeration ideas full time and gave up his medical practice. By 1850, he was producing blocks of artificial ice the size of bricks.

On May 6, 1851, U.S. Patent No. 8080, for a machine to make ice, was granted to Gorrie. He set out to find financial investors to manufacture his machine commercially. Unfortunately, Gorrie ran into intense opposition from investors and shippers of northern natural ice, as his ice machine threatened their financial interests. Frederick Tudor, dubbed the Ice King, who controlled a significant majority of the ice industry, surely did not want a modern mechanized processes to render his business obsolete, and he opposed Gorrie's invention. The *New York Globe* published an article asking, "This 'crank' down in Florida really thinks he can make ice with his ridiculous machine?" As a result, Gorrie failed to convince investors that his machine was feasible and potentially profitable and never managed to have it commercially manufactured.

Gorrie became financially ruined, was badgered by criticism and began suffering from declining heath. He died isolated from society on June 29, 1855, at the age of fifty-three.

NATIONAL STATUARY HALL COLLECTION

The National Statuary Hall Collection in the U.S. Capitol building in Washington, D.C., houses two statues from each of the fifty states. The statues are donated to honor notable people in each state's history. In 1914, the statue of John Gorrie was received by the National Statuary Hall Collection.

The other statue representing Florida is of Mary McLeod Bethune, civil rights activist, educator and presidential advisor; it was donated in 2022. Bethune was the first Black person represented in the National Statuary Hall Collection. Bethune's statue replaced one of Edmund Kirby Smith, a Confederate States of America army general, which was donated to the National Statuary Hall Collection in 1922. Smith's statue was removed in 2021 after much debate on the issue of Confederate memorials on public property.

The John Gorrie Museum State Park in Apalachicola displays a replica of his ice-making machine in the park's museum.

Model of Gorrie's first ice machine on display at the John Gorrie Museum, Apalachicola, Florida, circa 1958. *Courtesy of State Archives of Florida.*

CHAPTER 30

SOUTHERN DEMOCRAT TO REPUBLICAN STRONGHOLD STATE

From the end of Reconstruction in 1877 through 2025, thirty-four governors have held office in Florida. The majority, twenty-eight, were affiliated with the Democratic Party. The six who were not Democrats were Sidney J. Catts, who served from 1917 to 1921 as a member of the Prohibition Party, and Republicans Claude R. Kirk Jr., who served from 1967 to 1971; Jeb Bush (1999–2007); Charlie Christ (2007–11); Rick Scott (2011–19); and Ron DeSantis (2019–present).

Most of Florida's Democratic Party governors from 1877 through the 1960s were Southern Democrats and segregationists.

THE PORK CHOP GANG

Primarily active from the 1930s through the 1960s, a group of twenty Florida legislators, all members of the Democratic Party (Southern Democrats) representing rural areas in the northern part of the state, collaborated to dominate the Florida legislature. They were known as the Pork Chop Gang. They emulated McCarthyism, and their primary goals were to stop the civil rights movement, maintain racial segregation and protect the unequal political domination that favored the rural areas of northern Florida. They were able to obtain political domination because the state's legislative districts were not revised to account for the substantial urban population growth since the end of World War II. In 1960, Miami-Dade County had a

SOUTHERN DEMOCRATS

Before the American Civil War, most White men living in the Deep South were members of the Democratic Party, and they defended slavery and promoted its westward expansion. After the Reconstruction period ended in 1877, the southern wing of the Democratic Party became known as the Redeemers, who regained their political power by disenfranchising Blacks, establishing racial segregation and enforcing White supremacy. In 1948, Southern Democrats became angry with President Harry S. Truman (Democratic Party) as he enacted policies of desegregation, specifically Executive Order 9981, which mandated the desegregation of the U.S. military. Many Southern Democrats created a new party called the States Rights Democratic Party (commonly known as the Dixiecrats). The Dixiecrats Party was short-lived and collapsed in 1948 after Truman won the presidential election. In the 1960s, after President Lyndon B. Johnson (Democratic Party) signed major civil rights legislation, against heavy opposition from Southern Democrats, many White southerners changed their political affiliation to the Republican Party. The vast majority of today's Southern Democrats are more socially tolerant and progressive than their predecessors.

population of 935,047, and Jefferson County's population was only 9,543; however, both sent one senator to Florida's legislature. This politically unfair process meant that "12.3% of the population could elect a majority in the state senate and 14.7% could do the same in the lower house."

In 1956, the Pork Chop Gang organized the Johns Committee, which spent nine years investigating allegations of communist activities within the NAACP; no proof was ever unearthed. They also investigated allegations of subversive activities by academics, with an emphasis on homosexuality, in Florida's schools and universities. "By 1963, more than 39 college professors and deans had been dismissed from their positions at the three state universities, and 71 teaching certificates were revoked."

Florida's Constitution of 1968 finally revised the state's legislative districts based on population. This resulted in the Pork Chop Gang being thrown out of power in Florida.

Portrait of Florida's Pork Chop Gang, circa 1956. *Courtesy of Wikimedia Commons.*

FLORIDA BECOMES A REPUBLICAN PARTY–DOMINATED STATE

Since the 1994 Republican Revolution (when the Republican Party gained fifty-four seats in the House of Representatives and eight seats in the Senate during the midterm election), Florida has been trending toward being a Republican dominated state.

In 1999, Republican Party member Jeb Bush was elected governor. Since 1999, the four Florida governors have been members of the Republican Party.

As of this writing, Florida's Republican Party controls the offices of governor, secretary of state, and attorney general and both chambers of the state legislature. The Florida Senate has twenty-eight Republicans and twelve Democrats. The Florida House of Representatives has eighty-four Republicans and twelve Democrats. The Republican Party controls Florida's U.S. representatives as well: twenty out of twenty-eight U.S. House of Representative seats and both of the U.S. Senate seats.

CHAPTER 31

POPULATION GROWTH SINCE 1945

Florida's population has steadily grown since 1945, in part due to migration of "transplants" from other states and people from other Western Hemisphere countries, including Cuba and Haiti.

In 1945, Florida's population was 2.47 million. By the beginning of 2025, Florida's population is estimated to be 23 million. That is a population increase of 20.5 million since 1945, despite economic recessions, housing crises, pandemics and several destructive hurricane seasons.

Year	Florida's Population
2025	23,000,000 (estimated)
2020	21,569,932
2010	18,846,143
2000	16,047,515
1990	13,018,365
1980	9,839,835
1970	6,791,418
1960	5,004,000
1950	2,810,000
1945	2,465,000

Florida's population growth following 1945.

Many factors have contributed to population growth in Florida since 1945, including air-conditioning, cost of living, interstate highway construction, no state income tax, year-round warmer weather, Walt Disney World and tourism employment.

The cost of living in Florida is very close to the national average, which attracts new residents seeking affordable living expenses and, potentially, a higher quality of life. The lack of state income tax is also alluring for potential residents, especially retirees, as it increases spending power for individuals and families.

Interstate highways now span the state, stretching for 1,498 miles. The primary interstates are I-4, I-10, I-75, I-75E and I-95. The interstate system began in Florida in the late 1950s, making moving into and around the state faster and easier. Automobile transportation within the state has been dramatically improved since the 1950s, mainly due to the interstate highway system.

During the 1950s, air-conditioning was common in banks, commercial buildings, governmental facilities and hospitals. By the late 1960s, central air-conditioning was common in new houses, and window units were affordable for most older homes. Air-conditioning unquestionably makes living in a warm climate comfortable and more bearable.

The year-round warmer weather is perhaps the most alluring factor that brings new residents into Florida, many escaping harsh winters in northern states. The annual average temperature in Florida is 73.3 degrees Fahrenheit.

Walt Disney World generates $40 billion in economic impact, including direct and indirect tourism employment. Disney has a workforce of eighty-two thousand employees (one out of every thirty-two Florida jobs).

SENIOR CITIZENS AND FLORIDA'S GROWTH

As of this writing, Florida has more than 5.5 million residents aged sixty and older. The U.S. Census Bureau estimates that 32.5 percent of the state's population will exceed sixty years of age by 2030. Florida's Department of Elder Affairs defines a senior citizen as "someone who is 60 years of age or older." Perhaps the number one stereotype associated with Florida is its "old people."

FLORIDA'S BIRTH RATE IS DECLINING

Although Florida's population is soaring, its birth rate has been declining since 2007, dropping from 13.02 births per 1,000 people to 10.09 in 2022, a significant decrease of 22.5 percent. There were 224,433 live births in Florida in 2022. The total number of deaths in Florida was 238,953 in 2022, slightly higher than the number of births. Obviously, the catalyst of Florida's population growth is its migration.

CHAPTER 32

THE SPACE AGE

On October 4, 1957, the Union of Soviet Socialist Republics (USSR) successfully launched *Sputnik 1*, the world's first artificial satellite. This event spawned the Space Race, a twentieth-century rivalry between the United States and the USSR concentrating on spaceflight technology that became part of the Cold War. This was also the beginning of the Space Age (1957–present), the era of the exploration of space and its related technologies.

On October 1, 1958, the National Aeronautics and Space Administration (NASA) began operations. NASA is the independent U.S. governmental agency responsible for the civil space program and space research.

CAPE CANAVERAL

On March 7, 1962, NASA acquired land at Merritt Island (Cape Canaveral), which became its premier launch site for space missions. Cape Canaveral is now home to the Kennedy Space Center and the Cape Canaveral Space Force Station (CCSFS).

Starting in the early 1960s, Florida became a major player in the Space Age—Cape Canaveral being the hub. Thousands of new jobs, many relatively high-paying, in the fields of aeronautics, electrical and mechanical engineering, manufacturing and space research were the catalyst that relocated many new residents, many highly educated, into the state. The

The Apollo 10 Saturn V rocket shortly after rolling out from the rear of the Vehicle Assembly Building in Cape Canaveral, Florida, May 1969. *Courtesy of NASA.*

Cape Canaveral area, at one time, had the highest concentration of people with doctoral degrees in the nation.

Florida's rapid regional growth due to Space Age–related development spawned a housing boom in Brevard County, changing the area from predominantly agricultural to more suburban, with many more cultural and metropolitan-type facilities and activities. Attendance in Brevard County's school district quadrupled in size in the 1960s.

Florida's culture was changed by the Space Age, especially the Cape Canaveral area, which became known as the Space Coast. Many motels, restaurants, housing developments and bars decorated their establishments in space-age themes to attract tourists. Florida's tourist industry capitalized on the Space Age as many tourists traveled to Florida specifically to see modern space-related technology and rocket launches.

Economic and residential growth in Florida in the Daytona Beach, Cocoa Beach and Orlando areas was also attributed to Florida's Space Age–related development. As new defense contractors, high-tech manufacturing facilities and research labs spread throughout central Florida, Interstate 4 was constructed, linking the Space Coast area to the Tampa area. Interstate 4 is now a high-technology corridor.

NASA's space programs launched at Cape Canaveral included Gemini, Apollo (the most famous being Apollo 11, the spaceflight mission that was the first to land humans on the moon), Skylab and the Space Shuttle.

PRIVATE SPACE COMPANIES EMERGE

In 2011, the space shuttle program ended, and NASA and the Space Coast suffered an economic slowdown. Private companies—including SpaceX (an American spacecraft manufacturer, launch service provider and satellite communications company headquartered in Hawthorne, California), Blue Origin (an aerospace manufacturer, defense contractor, launch service provider and space technologies company headquartered in Kent, Washington), United Launch Alliance or ULA (an aerospace manufacturer, defense contractor and launch service provider headquartered in Centennial, Colorado) and the Boeing Company (a manufacturer of airplanes, missiles, rockets and satellites headquartered in Crystal City, Virginia)—have bolstered the Space Age industry in the Cape Canaveral area, elsewhere in Florida and around the nation.

SpaceX has used Cape Canaveral facilities to launch large numbers of spaceflights, including commercial and military satellites and crew and cargo missions to the International Space Station.

In 2020, SpaceX launched two NASA astronauts in a Falcon 9 rocket, a commercially owned spacecraft, from Cape Canaveral to the International

SpaceX's Falcon Heavy reusable side boosters land in unison at Cape Canaveral Landing Zones 1 and 2 following a test flight on February 6, 2018. *Courtesy of Wikimedia Commons.*

Space Station. This was the first time since 2011 that a human spaceflight was launched from U.S. soil and the first time NASA astronauts were placed into orbit in a commercially owned spacecraft.

On June 5, 2024, Boeing successfully launched two NASA astronauts on mission Crew Flight Test in a commercially owned Starliner spacecraft (a reusable spacecraft) from Cape Canaveral. Boeing is now competing with SpaceX's crewed Dragon spacecraft programs.

In 2024, NASA posted on its website that "it is enabling commercial industry to build, own, and operate space systems with the agency purchasing services for its science and research needs. Industry also can use those same services for fully commercial activities in space. Through our public-private partnerships, we are helping open space to more science, more people, and more opportunities."

Florida is benefiting from NASA's public-private collaboration as many more missions are being launched from Cape Canaveral and many more potential jobs and research opportunities are in the making.

CHAPTER 33

CUBAN MIGRATION

The Cuban Revolution began on July 26, 1953, with an assault led by Fidel Castro, a Cuban lawyer, Marxist-Leninist politician and radical revolutionist, on the Moncada Barracks, a military barracks in Santiago de Cuba. It ended on January 1, 1959, when U.S.-backed military dictator Fulgencio Batista was ousted and driven into exile in Portugal.

Cuba's new provisional government named Castro its prime minister. Castro had advocated for honest elections throughout the Cuban Revolution; however, once he seized power, such elections were squelched. Castro's government immediately conducted indiscriminate arrests and tortured and executed many people viewed as noncompliant with governmental policies. By May 15, 1959, approximately six hundred people had been executed by order of Castro's revolutionary courts.

Castro's oppressive one-party communist state has remained in power from 1959 to the present (even though Castro himself died in 2016 at age ninety).

LARGE EXODUSES OF CUBAN REFUGEES

THE CUBAN REVOLUTION (1953–59): Was responsible for launching a large exodus of refugees in 1959 as approximately two hundred thousand people fled to the United States. Since 1959, approximately 1.4 million Cuban refugees have entered the United States (the largest refugee flow in U.S.

history). Another three hundred thousand Cuban refugees fled to other countries in the Caribbean, Central and South America, Europe, Mexico and Canada.

OPERATION PETER PAN (1960–62): Over fourteen thousand unaccompanied Cuban children (mostly teenage boys) were covertly evacuated to the United States (most to the Miami area) by airplane to be looked after in federally funded foster care through what was called the Cuban Children's Program. The foster programs were managed by Father Bryan O. Walsh of the Catholic Welfare Bureau. Many Cuban parents were fearful of rumors that Castro was organizing "communist indoctrination centers" that were going to prohibit

Photograph of Fidel Castro, circa 1959. *Courtesy of Wikimedia Commons.*

religion and brainwash children with strict communist ideology. These centers were never known to be set up under the Castro regime.

Due to the Cuban Missile Crisis in October 1962, air traffic between Cuba and the United States was ended. This significantly limited opportunities for children to enter the United States under Operation Peter Pan.

FREEDOM FLIGHTS (1965–73): In December 1965, the Freedom Flights program was established, and almost three hundred thousand Cuban refugees were flown into the United States over the following eight years. Two flights a day departed from Varadero, Cuba. Most of the Cuban refugees boarding Freedom Flights were women or elderly people. Castro's regime placed migration restrictions on working-age men and skilled laborers, striving to keep most of them in the country.

The Catholic Welfare Bureau reported that about 90 percent of Operation Peter Pan's children were reunited with at least one of their parents as a result of this program.

MARIEL BOATLIFT (1980): This mass exodus started when Cuban citizens drove a bus through the gates of the Peruvian embassy in Havana and requested asylum. Castro removed all the Cuban guards from the embassy, and within a few days, over four thousand other asylum seekers sought refuge in the Peruvian embassy. Castro angrily announced, "Anyone who wants to leave Cuba can do so." He also called all Cuban asylum seekers "scum."

An exodus of asylum seekers, the majority of whom were adult males between twenty and thirty-four years old, flowed through the port of Mariel, Cuba. Scores of Cuban exiles assisted in organizing a flotilla of commercial shrimp boats and small private boats. The U.S. Coast Guard attempted to stop boats leaving the United States for Cuba. Despite the hastiness of the exodus and the U.S. Coast Guard's efforts, approximately 125,000 Cuban refugees entered the United States within a period of five months.

During the Mariel Boatlift, Castro discharged hospital patients and released prison inmates he termed "social undesirables," banishing them from Cuba. They were among the fleeing asylum seekers.

Of the 125,000 total refugees, it was estimated that 7,500 to 40,000 had criminal records in Cuba. Most of their criminal offences were not considered crimes in the United States; however, 1,774 were serious or violent offenders, and they were denied U.S. citizenship.

Established Cuban immigrants in the Miami area had doubts and suspicions about many Mariel Boatlift refugees, fearing their own status within the United States could be jeopardized. Concerns included some refugees' associations with the LGBTQ+ community and the *marielitos* (members of criminal gangs) who were among the Mariel Boatlift exiles.

Balseros, or the Cuban Raft Exodus (1994): After the collapse of the Soviet Union in 1991, financial aid coming into Cuba was severely reduced, which caused an economic recession, riots and civil unrest. Castro announced that

Two small boats in Florida waters overloaded with Cuban refugees during the Mariel boatlift in 1980. *Courtesy of Wikimedia Commons.*

anyone who wanted to leave Cuba could do so. Thousands of Cubans built makeshift rafts and began heading for the United States.

In order to avoid an unorganized and dangerous mass exodus, President Bill Clinton announced that these rafters would be detained by the U.S. Coast Guard and transferred to military bases at Guantánamo and Panama. More than thirty thousand Cuban refugees from the Balseros (Cuban Raft Exodus) were admitted into the United States.

As of January 2024, there are more than 2 million Cubans living in the United States. Cubans are the largest immigrant group from the Caribbean region and make up 4 percent of the Hispanic population in the United States. Cubans also make up 3 percent of all immigrants in the United States.

CHAPTER 34

WALT DISNEY WORLD

OPENING ON OCTOBER 1, 1971

According to Walt Disney and his brother Roy O. Disney, plans for what they called the "Florida project" began on November 15, 1965 during a press conference in Orlando. On October 27, 1966, Walt Disney released a film that revealed details and the location of a large new theme park to be constructed near Orlando. Disney said, "We have a perfect location in Florida, almost in the very center of the state. In fact, we selected this site because it is so easy for tourists and Florida residents to get here by automobile."

Only two months after Disney announced his visionary "Florida project," he died. Some talk about abandoning the project surfaced after Walt's death, but his older brother Roy took command. On May 30, 1967, the "Florida project" began, and Roy Disney announced it would be called Walt Disney World.

On October 1, 1971, the forty-seven-square-mile Walt Disney World officially opened. On October 25, 1971, Roy Disney read a dedication during the grand opening in which he said,

> Walt Disney World is a tribute to the philosophy and the life of Walter Elias Disney and to the talents and the dedication and the loyalty of the entire Disney organization that's made Walt Disney's dream come true.... May Walt Disney World bring joy and inspiration and new knowledge to all who come to this happy place. A Magic Kingdom where the young at heart of all ages can laugh and play and learn together.

The Magic Kingdom celebrated its twenty-fifth anniversary on October 1, 1996, with the largest anniversary confection ever. Cinderella Castle transformed the occasion and served as the backdrop and most memorable icon. Postcard circa 1996. *Author's collection.*

TREMENDOUS IMPACT ON FLORIDA

Walt Disney World has boosted Florida's economy and small businesses for more than fifty years, and it is now one of the most popular vacation destinations in the world. It averages fifty thousand visitors per day.

In 2022, Oxford Economics reported that the theme park generated $40 billion in economic impact and is responsible, directly and indirectly, for more than a quarter of a million jobs in Florida. This is approximately one out of every thirty-two jobs in Florida, which includes Disney's workforce of eighty-two thousand. Additionally, the report stated, "Disney is also vital to the funding of public services, as it generated taxes of $6.6 billion in 2022, including state and local taxes of $3.1 billion generated by Disney, non-local visitors, employees and third-party businesses—equivalent to $379 per Florida household."

BRIEF BIOGRAPHY OF WALTER ELIAS "WALT" DISNEY

Portrait of Walt Disney, circa 1954. *Courtesy of Wikimedia Commons.*

Walt Disney was born on December 5, 1901, in Chicago, Illinois, and died on December 15, 1966, in Burbank, California. He was a motion picture and television producer and a pioneering animated cartoon developer who created many famous characters, including Cinderella, Donald Duck, Goofy, Mickey Mouse, Snow White and Tinker Bell. Disney planned and supervised the construction of Disneyland, the legendary theme park in Anaheim, California. Construction of Disneyland began on July 21, 1954, and was completed on July 17, 1955. It has the largest cumulative attendance of all theme parks worldwide. Disney was also the visionary behind the larger theme park Walt Disney World, near Orlando, Florida. Walt Disney holds the record for the most Academy Awards won (twenty-six) and was honored with other prestigious awards, including three Golden Globes and one Emmy.

CHAPTER 35

HURRICANE ANDREW

On August 24, 1992, Hurricane Andrew made landfall in Florida (southern Miami-Dade County near Elliot Key) as a major Category 5 storm. According to the Saffir-Simpson Hurricane Wind Scale, a Category 5 storm produces winds of 157 miles per hour or higher and "catastrophic damage will occur: A high percentage of framed homes will be destroyed, with total roof failure and wall collapse. Fallen trees and power poles will isolate residential areas. Power outages will last for weeks to possibly months. Most of the area will be uninhabitable for weeks or months." At the time, Andrew was only the third Category 5 tropical cyclone to hit the United States; a fourth, Hurricane Michael, made landfall in Florida in 2018. Although Hurricane Andrew was compact in size, it was one of the strongest and costliest storms in the history of the United States, causing $26.5 billion in damage ($59.2 billion in 2025 dollars), fifteen direct deaths and twenty-eight indirect deaths in Florida. Hurricane Andrew quickly embedded itself in Florida's folklore as one of the state's most historic disasters.

In Florida, it is estimated that Hurricane Andrew damaged 101,241 homes and destroyed about 63,000 others; the majority of this destruction occurred in Miami-Dade County. About 1.4 million customers lost power, some for several months. South Miami neighborhoods endured massive destruction: 99 percent of the mobile homes in Miami-Dade County were destroyed, and tens of thousands of people in the county were left homeless.

Federal aid was initially slow in arriving to the ravaged areas, and Miami-Dade County Emergency Management director Kate Hale appeared

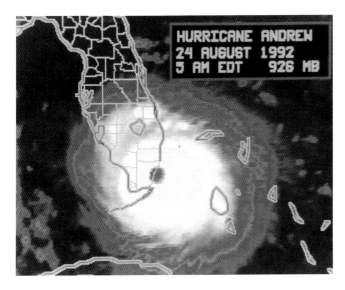

Satellite image of Hurricane Andrew shortly after landfall near Homestead, Florida. *Courtesy of Wikimedia Commons.*

frustrated on a nationally televised news conference, saying, "Where in the hell is the cavalry on this one? They keep saying we're going to get supplies. For God's sake, where are they?"

If the storm had stayed on its original projected course, its impact would have been significantly greater as it would have devastated major metropolitan areas, including the city of Miami.

STORY OF A SURVIVOR

Steve Warner, a psychologist who was hunkered down in a house in Redlands, Florida, during the fury of Hurricane Andrew, recalls,

> *It was quite an experience....You gain a whole new appreciation for the power of nature. When people say it sounds like a freight train, they're not exaggerating....The winds come with such force that it sounds like there is a freight train coming through the house. Everything was moved. Everything was destroyed. The paint came off the walls like sheets of wallpaper. I'd never seen anything like it before. The ceiling fan make a circular hole in the ceiling. The doors were blown off. The refrigerator had been pulled out of the kitchen. When we opened the door, we had seaweed in the refrigerator, and I know we hadn't bought any recently.*

THE AFTERMATH

Hurricane Andrew had many severe effects on Miami-Dade County. Demographics changed as thirty-six thousand people, the majority of them White, relocated in 1992, many to Broward and Palm Beach Counties. As high as 85 percent of fruit crops, including avocados, limes and mangoes, were destroyed. The crime rate rose; looting and theft were rampant immediately following the storm. A facility housing Burmese python snakes was destroyed, and many snakes escaped into the Everglades, where they have since multiplied significantly and are preying on native species. The economy of the southern part of Miami-Dade County lost many jobs as the U.S. Air Force Base in Homestead suffered catastrophic damage. It was partially rebuilt but reopened as the Homestead Air Reserve Base, which is only a fraction of the size of the original Air Force base. Even the Cleveland Indians (a major league baseball team) moved their spring training location out of Homestead to Winter Haven as many of their affluent fans relocated away from the Homestead area.

Serious psychological effects caused a rise in the divorce rate and cases of post-traumatic stress disorder (PTSD), especially among children. Eleven insurance companies went bankrupt, leaving more than 930,000 policyholders in South Florida without coverage. In order to restore adequate insurance coverage, the Florida legislature created the Joint Underwriting Association, the Florida Windstorm Underwriting Association and the Florida Hurricane Catastrophe Fund.

BUILDING CODES AND TECHNOLOGY IMPROVED

Structural damage caused by Hurricane Andrew revealed mediocre building techniques and exposed inadequate building code enforcement. Some roofs were built with cheap plywood and were attached with staples instead of nails. Both Miami-Dade and Broward Counties followed the South Florida Building Code standards, considered among the best in the country at the time. However, it was obvious that the codes were not being adequately enforced. Part of the problem was the area's rapid population growth in the 1970s and '80s, which tempted builders—and code enforcers—to cut corners. Proper adherence to the South Florida Building Code standards would have delayed many construction projects.

The Dadeland Mobile Home Park was thoroughly demolished by Hurricane Andrew. *Courtesy of Wikimedia Commons.*

When Hurricane Andrew devastated South Florida in 1992, the state had more than four hundred different building codes. In 2002, Florida enacted the Florida Building Code (FBC) statewide. The code "governs the design, construction, erection, alteration, modification, repair, and demolition of public and private buildings, structures, and facilities in the state." The code also identified the areas that are most prone to hurricanes and severe weather, which are called high-velocity hurricane zones (HVHZ).

Storm forecasting has significantly improved since Hurricane Andrew. Today, more sophisticated computers and many more satellites are used by meteorologists to collect and analyze data. Hurricane forecasts and warnings are broadcast quickly through traditional media outlets and through social media, which was not readily available in 1992. This new technology, along with more federal and state funding, allows people, communities and emergency management at the local, state and federal levels much more time to prepare and evacuate specific areas if necessary.

Since 1992, utility companies around the state have invested billions of dollars to improve power grids and other infrastructure. These improvements have led to faster storm recovery in areas that lose power caused by severe weather. Due to the lessons learned from Hurricane Andrew, Florida is now considered the nation's leader in emergency management and preparedness.

CHAPTER 36

PRESIDENTIAL ELECTION QUAGMIRES

Florida has been the focal point of two major contentious presidential elections that actually determined who became president of the United States. The first was the presidential election of 1876, in which Rutherford B. Hayes (the Republican party nominee and a Union military officer, member of the U.S. Congress and two-term governor of Ohio) was running against Samuel J. Tilden (the Democratic party nominee and the twenty-fifth governor of New York). The second was the infamous presidential election of 2000, in which George W. Bush (the Republican party nominee and the forty-sixth governor of Texas) was running against Albert A. Gore Jr. (the Democratic party nominee, forty-fifth vice president of the United States and senator from Tennessee).

RUTHERFORD B. HAYES VERSUS SAMUEL J. TILDEN (1876)

On Election Day, November 7, 1876, Samuel Tilden finished ahead of Rutherford B. Hayes by 260,000 votes, and it looked as though Tilden had the presidential election won. However, the electoral college votes in three states—Florida, Louisiana and South Carolina—were in doubt. Additionally, one of Oregon's three electoral votes, which was initially given to Tilden, was in doubt. Hayes was about to concede the election to Tilden, but William E. Chandler, a New Hampshire Republican leader, figured out that if Hayes were awarded all the doubtful electoral votes, he would be able to win the presidential election, 185 electoral votes to 184.

U.S. presidential candidates in 1876: Rutherford B. Hayes (*left*) and Samuel J. Tilden (*right*). *Courtesy of Wikimedia Commons.*

Both sides claimed victory, and Congress remained deadlocked over the results of the election into the following year. On January 29, 1877, Congress created an electoral commission to settle the dispute over the results. The commission included five members of the House of Representatives, five Senators and five Supreme Court justices. There were to be seven

Democrats, seven Republicans and one Independent. The Independent selected was Supreme Court Justice David Davis, but he refused to serve, and the other four justices appointed Supreme Court Justice Joseph P. Bradley, a Republican.

Justice Bradley originally was leaning toward Tilden as the winner of Florida's electoral votes but was persuaded to vote for Hayes. This early decision set a precedent for the electoral commission, which then voted along party lines, eight to seven, in favor of Hayes for the disputed electoral votes in Louisiana, South Carolina and Oregon. On March 2, 1877, Hayes was declared the winner of the 1876 presidential election by the narrowest of margins (185 to 184 electoral votes).

Threats of political violence and civil disobedience became a growing concern around the nation as many believed there was corruption involved in the electoral commission's decision to declare Hayes the winner.

THE COMPROMISE OF 1877

A secret, unwritten political deal to settle the congressional debate over the outcome of the 1876 presidential election and secure national political authority for Hayes is known as the Compromise of 1877, also known as the Wormley Agreement or the Bargain of 1877. To gain the support of Southern Democrats and obtain their promise to not block his election victory, Hayes secretly agreed to end the era of Reconstruction and withdraw federal troops from states still under military occupation.

Soon after President Hayes assumed office, he ended federal Reconstruction and enabled the federal government to adopt policies favorable to the South.

With the Southern Democrats back in power throughout the South and a lack of federal oversight, civil and political rights for African Americans and other people of color were largely ignored. Disenfranchisement of Black people became rampant, and Jim Crow racial segregation laws were passed in all Ssouthern states and some other states as well, where they were enforced until the modern Civil Rights Movement ended them in the 1960s.

GEORGE W. BUSH VERSUS AL GORE (2000)

In the presidential election of 2000, Al Gore gathered 540,000 more votes nationally than George W. Bush. However, the outcome of the election

U.S. presidential candidates in 2000: George W. Bush (*left*) and Al Gore (*right*). *Courtesy of Wikimedia Commons*.

depended on Florida's twenty-five electoral votes, and the state's election results were to "too close to call." The small margin—a 1,784 vote lead in favor of Bush—required a statewide machine recount under Florida's state law. The day following the election, automatic recounting started. Defective election administration in the state was exposed, and a full recount was never completed. The U.S. Supreme Court stepped in and made what many called a politicized decision, awarding Florida's electoral votes to George W. Bush, which secured him the victory in the 2000 presidential election.

On November 10, 2000, the statewide machine counts indicated that Bush's lead was only 327 votes. Gore requested a manual recount due to disputed ballots in four counties: Broward, Miami-Dade, Palm Beach and Volusia. These manual recounts were time-consuming and could not be completed by the original deadline. Gore sued to have the deadlines extended, while Bush's legal team attempted to stop the recount, stating that the recounts violated the Fourteenth Amendment because only four of Florida's sixty-seven counties were involved.

The recount exposed some irregular ballot issues in Florida. In Palm Beach County, the so-called butterfly ballot (a poorly designed ballot) that most likely caused at least 2,000 people in a heavily Democratic county to vote for Pat Buchanan, the Reform Party candidate. In Duval County, twenty-seven thousand votes in predominately Black precincts were classified as "overvotes" and nullified. These ballots reportedly had multiple markings, including two or more selections for president, as choices for president were listed on two non-facing pages.

Another election issue in Florida gained national attention: the secretary of state's office, prior to the 2000 presidential election, had ordered county officials to remove tens of thousands of felons from the voting rolls, a high percentage of whom were Black. It was discovered that at least 15 percent of the people removed were not felons and should have been eligible to vote.

On November 26, 2000, Katherine Harris, Florida's secretary of state, certified the statewide vote count, according to which Bush's lead was 537 votes. Appeals by both Bush and Gore were heard in the Florida Supreme Court and the U.S. Supreme Court.

U.S. SUPREME COURT CASE: *BUSH V. GORE* (2000)

Bush v. Gore, 531 U.S. 98 (2000) was argued on December 11, 2000, and decided on the same day. The primary holding of the case was: "Despite violating the Fourteenth Amendment by using disparate vote-counting procedures in different counties, Florida did not need to complete a recount in the 2000 presidential election because it could not be accomplished in a constitutionally valid way within the time limit set by federal law for resolving these controversies."

The election crisis, lasting more than a month, was ended by this U.S. Supreme Court decision, a 7–2 vote, which basically stated that the Florida Supreme Court's ruling requiring a statewide recount of ballots was unconstitutional.

On December 13, 2000, Gore, in a nationally televised address, conceded the election to Bush.

In the end, the 2000 presidential election was decided by only 537 votes in Florida, while an undetermined number of ballots were never recounted. This presidential election was the closest in U.S. history.

On January 20, 2001, George W. Bush was sworn in at the U.S. Capitol as the forty-third president of the United States.

BIBLIOGRAPHY

Chapter 1

Davis, Frederick T. "The Record of Ponce de Leon's Discovery of Florida, 1513." *Florida Historical Society Quarterly* 11, no. 1 (July 1932): 5–15.

Linden, Eugene. "The Vikings: A Memorable Visit to America." *Smithsonian Magazine*, December 2004.

Schultz, Colin. "Setting Sail: the 500th Anniversary of Juan Ponce de León's Discovery of Florida." *Smithsonian Magazine*, March 27, 2013. www.smithsonianmag.com.

Shaer, Matthew. "Ponce De Leon Never Searched for the Fountain of Youth." *Smithsonian Magazine*, June 2013. www.smithsonianmag.com.

Tebeau, Charlton W. *A History of Florida*. University of Miami Press, 1971.

Turner, Samuel. "Juan Ponce de León and the Discovery of Florida Reconsidered." *Florida Historical Quarterly* 92, no. 1 (Summer 2013): 1–31.

Chapter 2

Goodwin, R.T.C. "'De lo que sucedió a los demás que entraron en las Indias': Álvar Núñez Cabeza de Vaca and the Other Survivors of Pánfilo Narváez's Expedition." *Bulletin of Spanish Studies: Hispanic Studies and Researches on Spain, Portugal and Latin America* 84, no. 2 (2007): 147–73.

Goodwyn, Frank. "Pánfilo de Narváez, a Character Study of the First Spanish Leader to Land an Expedition to Texas." *Hispanic American Historical Review* 29, no. 1 (February 1949): 150–56.

Milanich, Jerald T. *Florida Indians and the Invasion from Europe*. University Press of Florida, 1995.

Minster, Christopher. "Explorer Pánfilo de Narváez Found Disaster in Florida."
    ThoughtCo., October 28, 2019. www.thoughtco.com.

Oviedo y Valdez, Gonzalo Fernandez, and Harbert Davenport. "The Expedition
    of Pánfilo de Narváez." *Southwestern Historical Quarterly* 27, no. 2 (October 1923):
    120–39.

Resendez, Andres. "Cabeza de Vaca and the Problem of First Encounters."
    Historically Speaking 10, no. 1 (January 2009): 36–38.

Schneider, Paul. *Brutal Journey: The Epic Story of the First Crossing of North America.*
    Henry Holt, 2006.

Worth, John E. *Discovering Florida: First-Contact Narratives from Spanish Expeditions Along
    the Lower Gulf Coast.* University of Florida Press, 2014.

Chapter 3

Boyd, Mark F. "The Arrival of De Soto's Expedition in Florida." *Florida Historical
    Quarterly* 16, no. 3, (January 1938): 188–220.

Duncan, David Ewing. *Hernando de Soto: A Savage Quest in the Americas.* University of
    Oklahoma Press, 1996.

Fox News. "Archaeologist Uncovers Evidence of Hernando de Soto's Expedition."
    January 10, 2017. www.foxnews.com.

Irving, Theodore. *The Conquest of Florida, Under Hernando de Soto.* Carey, Lea &
    Blanchard, 1835.

Milanich, Jerald T. *Florida Indians and the Invasion from Europe.* University Press of
    Florida, 1995.

Schneider, Paul. *Brutal Journey: The Epic Story of the First Crossing of North America.*
    Henry Holt, 2006.

Swanton, John R. "De Soto's First Headquarters in Florida." *Florida Historical
    Quarterly* 30, no. 4 (April 1952): 311–16.

———. *Final Report of the United States De Soto Expedition Commission.* Smithsonian
    Institution Press, 1985.

Chapter 4

Covington, James W. "Migration of the Seminoles into Florida, 1700–1820."
    Florida Historical Quarterly 46, no. 4 (April 1968): 340–57.

Dysart, Jane E. "Another Road to Disappearance: Assimilation of Creek Indians in
    Pensacola, Florida, During the Nineteenth Century." *Florida Historical Quarterly*
    61, no. 1 (July 1982): 37–48.

Ehrmann, W.W. "The Timucua Indians of Sixteenth Century Florida." *Florida
    Historical Quarterly* 18, no. 3 (January 1940): 168–91.

Gold, Robert L. "The East Florida Indians Under Spanish and English Control: 1763–1765." *Florida Historical Quarterly* 44, no. 1, Quadricentennial Edition (July–October 1965): 105–20.

Mehta, Jayur Madhusadan, and Tara Skipton. "Florida's Indigenous Heritage Faces a Watery Grave." *Sapiens Anthropology Magazine*, October 11, 2019. www.sapiens.org.

Milanich, Jerald T. *Florida Indians and the Invasion from Europe.* University Press of Florida, 1995.

Schneider, Paul. *Brutal Journey: The Epic Story of the First Crossing of North America.* Henry Holt, 2006.

Wilkinson, Jerry. "Historic Florida Indians." Keyhistory.org. http://www.keyshistory.org.

Chapter 5

Arnade, Charles W. "Tristán de Luna and Ochuse (Pensacola Bay) 1559." *Florida Historical Quarterly* 37, no. 3 (January–April 1959): 201–22.

Gonzalez, S.J. "Pensacola: Its Early History." *Florida Historical Quarterly* 2, no. 1 (April 1909): 9–25.

Griffen, William B. "Spanish Pensacola, 1700–1763." *Florida Historical Quarterly* 37, no. 3 (January–April 1959): 242–62.

Hudson, Charles, Marvin T. Smith, Chester B. DePratter and Emilia Kelley. "The Tristán de Luna Expedition, 1559–1561." *Southeastern Archaeology* 8, no. 1 (Summer 1989): 31–45.

Lloyd, Robert B., Jr. "Development of the Plan of Pensacola During the Colonial Era, 1559–1821." *Florida Historical Quarterly* 64, no. 3 (January 1986): 253–72.

Priestley, Herbert Ingram. *Tristan De Luna, Conquistador of the Old South: A Study of Spanish Imperial Strategy.* Porcupine Press, 1980.

Webster, Donovan. "Harboring History in Pensacola." *Smithsonian Magazine*, May 2009. www.smithsonianmag.com.

Chapter 6

Arana, Luis Rafael. "The Exploration of Florida and Sources on the Founding of St. Augustine." *Florida Historical Quarterly* 44, no. 1 (July–October 1965): 1–16.

Connolly, Matthew J. "Four Contemporary Narratives of the Founding of St. Augustine." *Catholic Historical Review* 51, no. 3 (October 1965): 305–34.

Covington, James W. "Drake Destroys St. Augustine: 1586." *Florida Historical Quarterly* 44, no. 1, (July–October 1965): 81–93.

Gorman, M. Adele Francis. "Jean Ribault's Colonies in Florida" *Florida Historical Quarterly* 44, no. 1 (July–October 1965): 51–66.

Griffin, Patricia. "Penon Inlet and the Massacre of the French." *St. Augustine Archaeological Association Newsletter* 22, no. 1 (February 2007).

Lyon, Eugene. "The Captives of Florida." *Florida Historical Quarterly* 50, no. 1 (July 1971): 1–24.

———. "Pedro Menéndez's Strategic Plan for the Florida Peninsula." *Florida Historical Quarterly* 67, no. 1 (July 1988): 1–14.

McGrath, John T. "Admiral Coligny, Jean Ribault, and the East Coast of North America." *French Colonial History* 1 (2002): 63–76.

———. "A Massacre Revised: Matanzas, 1565." *Proceedings of the Meeting of the French Colonial Historical Society* 21, Essays in French Colonial History (1997): 15–29.

Waterbury, Jean Parker, ed. *The Oldest City: St. Augustine, Saga of Survival*. St. Augustine Historical Society, 1983.

Chapter 7

Arnade, Charles W. "Cattle Raising in Spanish Florida, 1513–1763." *Agricultural History* 35, no. 3 (July 1961): 116–24.

Clements, Sid. "Indian Cowboys: Home of the Reservation Range." *Tampa Bay Times*, April 25, 1976.

Miami Herald. "1,250,000 Cattle Graze on Florida's Plains as Stock Rises to High Standard of Quality." June 5, 1938.

News Press. "Cattle Tradition Blooms." December 10, 1995.

Schumann, F. "Much of State Foundation Laid by Cattlemen." *Orlando Evening Star*, March 22, 1931.

Taylor, Robert A. "Rebel Beef: Florida Cattle and the Confederate Army, 1862–1864." *Florida Historical Quarterly* 67, no. 1 (July 1988): 15–31.

VanLandingham, Kyle S. "Captain William B. Hooker: Florida Cattle King." *Sunland Tribune* 22 (1996).

Yariett, Lewis L. "History of the Florida Cattle Industry." *Rangelands* 7, no. 5 (October 1985): 205–07.

Chapter 8

Landers, Jane. "Spanish Sanctuary: Fugitives in Florida, 1687–1790." *Florida Historical Quarterly* 62, no. 3 (January 1984): 296–313.

Lennox, Lisa. "Florida's Culture of Slavery." Florida Humanities, February 24, 2020. https://floridahumanities.org.

Mormino, Gary. "Want to Know About Slavery in Florida? Listen to Former Slaves." *Tampa Bay Times*, August 3, 2023. https://www.tampabay.com.

PBS. "Why Slaves Escaped to Florida for Asylum." https://www.pbs.org.

Riordan, Patrick. "Finding Freedom in Florida: Native Peoples, African Americans, and Colonists, 1670–1816." *Florida Historical Quarterly* 75, no. 1 (Summer 1996): 24–43.

Chapter 9

Deagan, Kathleen A., and Darcie A. MacMahon. *Fort Mose: Colonial America's Black Fortress of Freedom.* University Press of Florida, 1995.

Florida Museum. "Fort Mose: America's Black Colonial Fortress of Freedom." https://www.floridamuseum.ufl.edu.

Fort Mose Historical Society. "The Fort Mose Story." https://fortmose.org.

London, Aaron. "Fort Mose: America's First Free Black Town." *Evolve Magazine.* https://evolve-success.com.

UNESCO Sites of Memory. "Fort Mose." https://unescositesofmemory.org.

Chapter 10

Neale, Rick. "Ceremony to Mark Revolutionary War's Final Naval Battle from 1783 near Cape Canaveral." *Florida Today*, March 14, 2023. https://www.floridatoday.com.

St. Augustine Historical Society. "British Florida Historical Resources." https://staughs.com.

Witcher, T.R. "Pioneering Pathway: The King's Road." *Civil Engineering* (December 2019): 36–39.

Wright, J. Leitch, Jr. "Blacks in British East Florida." *Florida Historical Quarterly* 54, no. 4 (April 1976): 425–42.

Chapter 11

Carita, Doggett. *Dr. Andrew Turnbull and the New Smyrna Colony of Florida.* Heritage Books, 2013.

Florida History Online. "Smyrnéa: Dr. Andrew Turnbull and the Mediterranean Settlement." https://history.domains.unf.edu.

Florida Memory. "Dr. Andrew Turnbull and the Origins of New Smyrna Beach." May 5, 2014. https://www.floridamemory.com.

New Smyrna Museum of History. "The Turnbull Settlement 'Smyrnea.'" https://nsbhistory.org.

Chapter 12

Cusick, James G. *The Other War of 1812: The Patriot War and the American Invasion of Spanish East Florida*. University of Georgia Press, 2007.

Kruse, Paul. "A Secret Agent in East Florida: General George Mathews and the Patriot War." *Journal of Southern History* 18, no. 2 (May 1952): 193–217.

Patrick, Rembert W. *Florida Fiasco: Rampant Rebels on the Georgia-Florida Border, 1810–1815*. University of Georgia Press, 1954.

Porter, Kenneth Wiggins. "Negroes and the East Florida Annexation Plot, 1811–1813." *Journal of Negro History* 30, no. 1 (January 1945): 9–29.

Stagg, J.C.A., James Madison and George Mathews: "The East Florida Revolution of 1812 Reconsidered." *Diplomatic History* 30, no. 1 (January 2006): 23–55.

Troxler, Carole Watterson. "Refuge, Resistance, and Reward: The Southern Loyalists' Claim on East Florida." *Journal of Southern History* 55, no. 4 (November 1989): 563–96.

Chapter 13

Covington, James W. "Migration of the Seminoles into Florida, 1700–1820." *Florida Historical Quarterly* 46, no. 4 (April 1968): 340–57.

Kleinberg, Eliot. "The Most Expensive War the White Man Ever Waged Against Native Americans." *Palm Beach Post*, February 28, 2019.

Missall, John, and Mary Lou Missall. *The Seminole Wars: America's Longest Indian Conflict*. University Press of Florida, 2004.

National Park Service. "Seminole Incarceration." https://www.nps.gov.

Sarasota Herald-Tribune. "Jackson Launched Controversial First Seminole War in Florida in 1818." December 12, 2002. https://www.heraldtribune.com.

Weisman, Brent R. "The Background and Continued Cultural and Historical Importance of the Seminole Wars in Florida." *FIU Law Review* 9, no. 2: 391–404.

Wright, J. Leitch, Jr. "A Note on the First Seminole War as Seen by the Indians, Negroes, and Their British Advisers." *Journal of Southern History* 34, no. 4 (November 1968): 565–75.

Chapter 14

Martin, Sidney Walter. "Richard Keith Call, Florida Territorial Leader." *Florida Historical Quarterly* 21, no. 4 (April 1943): 332–51.

Moussalli, Stephanie D. "Florida's Frontier Constitution: The Statehood, Banking & Slavery Controversies." *Florida Historical Quarterly* 74, no. 4 (Spring 1996): 423–39.

National Park Service. "The Second Spanish Period (1784–1821)." https://www.nps.gov.

P.K. Younge Library of Florida History. "1821: Florida Becomes Part of the United States." August 20, 2021. https://pkyonge.uflib.ufl.edu/2021/08/20/1821-florida-becomes-part-of-the-united-states/

Tebeau, Charlton W. *A History of Florida*. University of Miami Press, 1987.

Chapter 15

Florida Memory. "Florida in the Civil War: Ordinance of Secession, 1861." https://www.floridamemory.com.

Florida Timeline. "1861: Florida Secedes Over Slavery and Joins the Confederacy." https://www.floridatimeline.org.

Jones, Allen W. "Military Events in Florida During the Civil War, 1861–1865." *Florida Historical Quarterly* 39, no. 1 (July 1960): 42–45.

Reiger, John F. "Deprivation, Disaffection, and Desertion in Confederate Florida." *Florida Historical Quarterly* 48, no. 3 (January 1970): 279–98.

Wooster, Ralph A. "The Florida Secession Convention." *Florida Historical Quarterly* 36, no. 4 (April 1958): 373–85.

Chapter 16

Chafe, William H., ed. *Remembering Jim Crow: African Americans Tell About Life in the Segregated South*. New Press, 2001.

Clark, James C. "Lynching: Florida's Brutal Distinction." *Orlando Sentinel*, March 7, 1993. https://www.orlandosentinel.com.

Florida Historical Society. "Ax Handle Saturday." https://myfloridahistory.org.

Gardner, Sheldon. "St. Augustine's Civil Rights Movement: A Look at Dr. Martin Luther King Jr.'s Legacy." *St. Augustine Record*, January 18, 2021. https://www.staugustine.com.

Jaye, Randy. *Perseverance: Episodes of Black History from the Rural South*. Self-published, 2020.

New York Times. "Dr. King Describes St. Augustine as Most Lawless City He's Seen; Reports Threats on His Life in Florida—Shots Are Fired Into a Negro's Automobile." June 6, 1964. https://www.nytimes.com.

Pegoda, Andrew Joseph. "What People Still Get Wrong About Segregation." *Time*, February 3, 2020. https://time.com.

Sharp, Anne Wallace. *A Dream Deferred: The Jim Crow Era*. Lucent Books, 2005.

Uhl, Sadie, and Hope Evans. "The Story of the Tallahassee Bus Boycott." Florida State University Department of History, February 6, 2021. https://history.fsu.edu.

Chapter 17

Brown, Jeff. "End of the Line: The Overseas Railway." *Civil Engineering* (June 2014): 46–49.

Corliss, Carlton J. "Henry M. Flagler: Railroad Builder." *Florida Historical Quarterly* 38, no. 3 (January 1960): 195–205.

Perez, Amanda M. "Flagler's Journey to Florida." University of Miami, September 16, 2019. https://news.miami.edu.

Turkel, Stanley. "Henry Morrison Flagler: The Man Who Invented Florida." *Cornell Hotel and Restaurant Administration Quarterly* (April 1998): 76–79.

Wilkinson, Jerry. "History of the Railroad." KeysHistory.org. https://www.keyshistory.org.

Chapter 18

Florida Historical Society. "Florida Frontiers 'Henry B. Plant.'" https://myfloridahistory.org.

Johnson, Dudley S. "Henry Bradley Plant and Florida." *Florida Historical Quarterly* 45, no. 2 (October 1966): 118–31.

Opal Collection. "Henry Plant: The Florida Legend You Never Knew." https://www.opalcollection.com.

Tampa Magazine. "Tampa Icons: Henry B. Plant (1819–1899)." June 14, 2018. https://tampamagazines.com.

Chapter 19

Gross, David. "How 1910s Los Angeles Surpassed Jacksonville as the Movie Industry's Warm Weather Capital." Medium, March 10, 2020. https://whyisthereacitythere.medium.com.

Hamilton, Bruce. "Lights, Camera, Action! Jacksonville Was America's First Hollywood." News4Jax.com, May 5, 2022. https://www.news4jax.com.

Herman, Carolyn. "'Lights, Camera, Action!' The Role of Jacksonville in the Silent Film Era." *Trust the Leaders* no. 38 (Summer 2015): 14–16. https://www.sgrlaw.com.

Norman Studios. "Preserving Jacksonville's Silent Film Legacy." http://normanstudios.org.

Soergel, Matt. "Want to Watch Some of the Old Silent Films Shot in Jacksonville? Here Are 20 of Them." *Florida Times-Union*, March 16, 2022. https://www.jacksonville.com.

TheCoastal.com. "'Winter Film Capital of the World': The Early Cinematic History of Jacksonville." May 11, 2020. https://thecoastal.com.

Williams, Cynthia. "Florida History: Jacksonville's Role in the Silent Film Industry." *News-Press*, September 26, 2021. https://www.news-press.com.

Chapter 20

Anderson, Curt. "Pollution from Florida's Phosphate Mining Industry a Concern with Hurricane Ian." Associated Press, September 28, 2022.

Cooper, Julia. "Florida's Hidden Backbone." WUFT. https://projects.wuft.org.

Dunn History. "The Brutality of Florida's Turpentine Industry." https://dunnhistory.com.

Florida Citrus. "Citrus Arrived in America in the Early 1500s but Wasn't Grown Commercially Until the 1800s." https://www.floridacitrus.org/about-florida-citrus/our-history/

Florida Historical Society. "The Sugarcane Saga." https://myfloridahistory.org.

Florida Memory. "Bittersweet: The Rise and Fall of the Citrus Industry in Florida." https://www.floridamemory.com.

Mitchell, Scott. "The Sweet History of Sugarcane." *Ocala Style*, August 1, 2022. https://www.ocalastyle.com.

Morse, Hannah. "How the Sugar Industry Makes Political Friends and Influences Elections." *Palm Beach Post*, February 3, 2022. https://www.palmbeachpost.com.

Newborn, Steve. "History of Phosphate Mining in Florida Fraught with Peril." *WUSF*, June 16, 2021. https://www.wusf.org.

Chapter 21

Florida Memory. "Florida in World War I." https://www.floridamemory.com.

Mormino, Gary R. "All Disquiet on the Home Front: World War I and Florida, 1914–1920." *Florida Historical Quarterly* 97, no. 3 (Winter 2019): 249–99.

Tebeau, Charlton W. *A History of Florida*. University of Miami Press, 1987.

U.S. Caribbean & Florida Digital Newspaper Project. "When It Was Over Over There: Florida Soldiers and the End of World War I." November 9, 2018. https://ufndnp.domains.uflib.ufl.edu.

Chapter 22

Calvan, Caina Bobby. "As Racism Protests Roil U.S., Florida Revisits Dark Past." Associated Press, June 20, 2020. www.apnews.com.

Florida Senate. "CS/CS/HB 1213: Educational Instruction of Historical Events." www.flsenate.gov.

Hudak, Stephen. "Downtown Marker Memorializes July Perry, Lynched in Orlando Nearly a Century Ago." *Orlando Sentinel*, June 21, 2019. www.orlandosentinel.com.

McLeod, Michael, and Joy Wallace Dickinson. "Ocoee Race Riot Scars Generations." *Orlando Sentinel*, February 5, 2001. www.orlandosentinel.com.

Miami Herald. "Number of Dead in Ocoee Not Known." November 4, 1920.

Ocala Evening Star. "Ocoee's Deplorable Affair." November 6, 1920.

Orlando Sentinel. "As Negro Houses Burned at Ocoee Great Mass of Ammunition Is Exploded." November 4, 1920.

Ortiz, Paul. *Emancipation Betrayed: The Hidden History of Black Organizing and White Violence in Florida from Reconstruction to the Bloody Election of 1920.* University of California Press, 2005.

———. "Ocoee, Florida: Remembering 'The Single Bloodiest Day in Modern U.S. Political History.'" *Facing South*, May 14, 2010. https://www.facingsouth.org.

Tampa Tribune. "2 Whites Killed, 3 Wounded, Near Ocoee." November 3, 1920.

Toohey, Grace. "New Florida Law to Teach, Recognize 1920 Ocoee Massacre That Destroyed City's Black Community." *Orlando Sentinel*, June 24, 2020. www.orlandosentinel.com.

Chapter 23

FloridaHistory.org. "Florida in the 1920s: The Great Florida Land Boom." https://floridahistory.org.

Kleinberg, Eliot. "The Role of the 'Binder Boys' in the Land Boom of the 1920s." *Palm Beach Post*, December 12, 2021. https://www.palmbeachpost.com.

Turner, Gregg M. *The Florida Land Boom of the 1920s.* McFarland, 2015.

Vanderblue, Homer B. "The Florida Land Boom." *Journal of Land & Public Utility Economics* 3, no. 3 (August 1927): 252–69.

Chapter 24

Brouchu, Nicole. "Florida's Forgotten Storm: The Hurricane of 1928." *Sun Sentinel*, August 23, 2019.

Bunting, Donald C. "A Comparison of Six Great Florida Hurricanes." *Weatherwise* (June 1955): 64–82.

Kleinberg, Eliot. "Florida Time: Why Did 600+ Black People Get Buried in an Unmarked Grave?" *Palm Beach Post*, June 6, 2019. https://www.palmbeachpost.com.

PBS. "The Okeechobee Hurricane 1928." https://www.pbs.org.

Pfost, Russell L. "Reassessing the Impact of Two Historical Florida Hurricanes." *American Meteorological Society* (October 2003): 1367–72.

Chapter 25

Brieskorn, Katlyn. "9 Things to Know About Florida During the Great Depression." WFTV, May 10, 2020. https://www.wftv.com.

Cox, Merlin G. "David Sholtz: New Deal Governor of Florida." *Florida Historical Quarterly* 43, no. 2 (October 1964): 142–52.

Living New Deal. "Florida Sites." https://livingnewdeal.org.

Tebeau, Charlton W. *A History of Florida*. University of Miami Press, 1987.

Chapter 26

Drye, Willie. "The True Story of the Most Intense Hurricane You've Never Heard Of." *National Geographic*, September 8, 2017. https://www.nationalgeographic.com.

Hurricanescience.org. "1935: Labor Day Hurricane." https://hurricanescience.org.

Mann, Randi. "Recalling the Catastrophic 1935 Labor Day Hurricane—Battered the Florida Keys." Weather Network, September 2, 2021. https://www.theweathernetwork.com.

Space Coast Daily. "1935 Labor Day Hurricane That Hit Florida Keys Was First Known Category 5 On Record to Strike the Contiguous U.S." September 3, 2023. https://spacecoastdaily.com.

Chapter 26

Florida Memory. "Florida in World War II." https://www.floridamemory.com.

Guzzo, Paul. "Nazi Submarines Brought the Fight to Florida During WWII." *Tampa Bay Times*, September 15, 2020. https://www.tampabay.com.

Miller, Donald L. *The Story of World War II*. Simon & Schuster, 2001.

Museum of Florida History. "Florida on the Home Front: The German Submarine Threat off Florida's Coast." https://www.museumoffloridahistory.com.

Chapter 28

Dovell, Junius E. "The Everglades, a Florida Frontier. Agricultural History Society." *Agricultural History* 22, no. 3 (July 1948): 187–97.

Florida Fish and Wildlife Conservation Commission. "Everglades: History." https://myfwc.com.

Gunderson, Lance H., Stephen S. Light and C.S. Holling. "Lessons from the Everglades." In "Science and Biodiversity Policy." Supplement, *BioScience* 45 (1995): S66–S73.

National Park Service. "History & Culture." https://www.nps.gov.

Chapter 29

Florida State Parks. "John Gorrie Museum State Park." https://www.floridastateparks.org.

Henderson, Alfred R. "John Gorrie, MD, 1803–1855: Pioneer of Air Conditioning and Refrigeration." *JAMA* (July 27, 1963): 330–33.

National Museum of American History. "Gorrie Ice Machine, Patent Model." https://americanhistory.si.edu.

Roth, George B. "Dr. John Gorrie: Inventor of Artificial Ice and Mechanical Refrigeration." *Scientific Monthly* 42, no. 5 (May 1936): 464–69.

Chapter 30

Colburn, David R. *From Yellow Dog Democrats to Red State Republicans: Florida and Its Politics Since 1940.* University Press of Florida, 2007.

Greenwood, Max. "How Florida Became a Conservative Bastion." The Hill, May 15, 2023. https://thehill.com.

Miller, James Nathan. "How Florida Threw Out the Pork Chop Gang." *National Civic Review* (July 1971): 366–71, 380.

Mohammad, Linah, Patrick Jarenwattananon and Eliss Nadworny. "How Florida, a One-Time Swing State, Turned Red." NPR, November 10, 2022. https://www.npr.org.

Weitz, Seth A. *Bourbon, Pork Chops, and Red Peppers: Political Immorality in Florida, 1945–1968.* Florida State University, 2007.

Chapter 31

CBS News. "Expert on Florida Population Growth: It's the Highest Number It's Ever Been." December 7, 2023. https://www.cbsnews.com.

Senior Consulting Advisors. "5 Reasons Why Florida Is a Great Place to Retire." https://floridaseniorconsulting.com.

Smith, Stanley K. "Florida Population Growth: Past, Present and Future." University of Florida Bureau of Economic and Business Research, June 2005. https://www.bebr.ufl.edu.

Wunderlich, Emily. "Seniors Drive Florida Population Growth, Study Shows." *Sarasota Herald-Tribune*, June 19, 2019. https://www.heraldtribune.com.

Chapter 32

Blake, Talia. "To Infinity and Beyond: How Space Impacts Florida's Economy." *Central Florida Public Media*, October 3, 2023. https://www.cfpublic.org.

Bliss, Laura. "Will Florida Get Pushed Out of the New Space Age?" *Bloomberg*, August 7, 2014. https://www.bloomberg.com.

Feldscher, Jacqueline. "SpaceX Makes History with Launch of Astronauts." Politico, May 30, 2020. https://www.politico.com.

Florida Space Institute. "Accelerating Space Research and Education." https://fsi.ucf.edu.

NASA. "Kennedy Space Center History." https://www.nasa.gov.

Patrick, Craig. "How the Space Program Launched the Florida We Know Today." Fox 13 News, July 19, 2019. https://www.fox13news.com.

Wattles, Jackie, Ashley Stickland and Maureen Chowdhury. "Boeing Launches First Crewed Starliner Spacecraft." CNN, June 5, 2024. https://www.cnn.com.

Chapter 33

Brown, Joel. "Why Is the Cuban Immigrant Story in the U.S. So Different from Others?" Boston University, August 1, 2022. https://www.bu.edu.

Duany, Jorge. "Cuban Migration: A Post-Revolution Exodus Ebbs and Flows." Migration Policy Institute, July 6, 2017. https://www.migrationpolicy.org.

Gutierrez, Lizbeth. "Breaking Down South Florida's Record Cuban Immigration Numbers." Bay News 9, April 27, 2024. https://baynews9.com.

Larzelere, Alex. *Castro's Ploy—America's Dilemma: The 1980 Cuban Boatlift*. National Defense University Press, 1988.

Skop, Emily H. "Race and Place in the Adaption of Muriel Exiles." *International Migration Review* 35, no. 2 (Summer 2001): 449–71.

Chapter 34

Flaherty, Morgan. "How Walt Disney World Became the Theme Park Capital of the World." All Ears, April 7, 2020. https://allears.net.

Fox 35 Orlando. "The History of Walt Disney World and Its Opening 50 Years Ago." October 1, 2021. https://www.fox35orlando.com.

Izard, Ralph S. "Walt Disney: Master of Laughter and Learning." *Peabody Journal of Education* (November 4, 2009): 36–41.

MagicGuides.com. "Disney World History: Discover the Fascinating History Behind Walt Disney World Resort." https://magicguides.com.

Potter, Derek. "Theme Park History: Walt Disney and the Beginning of His 'World.'" Theme Park Insider, December 15, 2013. https://www.themeparkinsider.com.

Watts, Steven. "Walt Disney: Art and Politics in the American Century." *Journal of American History* 82, no. 1 (June 1995): 84–110.

Chapter 35

Christie, John, ed. *Andrew! Savagery from the Sea.* Tribune Publishing, 1992.

Insurance Information Institute. "Hurricane Andrew Fact Sheet." https://www.iii.org.

Jacobo, Julia. "Hurricane Andrew 25 Years Later: The Monster Storm That Devastated South Miami." ABC News, August 24, 2017. https://abcnews.go.com.

Smith, Stanley K., and Christopher McCarty. "Demographic Effects of Natural Disasters: A Case Study of Hurricane Andrew." *Demography* 33, no. 2 (May 1996): 265–75.

Willoughby, H.E., and P.G. Black. "Hurricane Andrew in Florida: Dynamics of a Disaster." *Bulletin of the American Meteorological Society* 77, no. 3 (March 1996): 543–49.

Zhang, Yang, and Walter Gillis Peacock. "Planning for Housing Recovery? Lessons Learned from Hurricane Andrew." *Journal of the American Planning Association* 76, no. 1 (Winter 2010): 5–24.

Chapter 36

Blackford, Sheila. "Disputed Election 1876: The Death Knell of the Republican Dream." Miller Center. https://millercenter.org.

Elving, Ron. "The Florida Recount of 2000: A Nightmare That Goes On Haunting." NPR, November 12, 2018. https://www.npr.org.

Leib, Jonathan I., and Jason Dittmer. "Florida's Residual Votes, Voting Technology, and the 2000 Election." *Political Geography* 21 (2002): 91–98.

Lewis, Walker. "The Hayes-Tilden Election." *American Bar Association Journal* 47, no. 1 (January 1961): 36–40.

Mebane, Walter. "The Wrong Man Is President! Overvotes in the 2000 Presidential Election in Florida." *Perspectives on Politics* 2, no. 3 (September 2004): 525–35.

Pickett, Alex. "Florida's Long, Long History of Election Woes." Courthouse News Service, November 16, 2018. https://www.courthousenews.com.

Shofner, Jerrell H. "Fraud and Intimidation in the Florida Election of 1876." *Florida Historical Quarterly* 42, no. 4 (April 1964): 321–30.

ABOUT THE AUTHOR

Randy Jaye has had a lifelong interest in and passion for history. He has traveled extensively visiting, researching and photographing historic sites, museums and historical societies. He believes that studying history helps people understand how past events have shaped the present. He is also a firm believer that understanding the lessons of history can prevent undesirable events in our past from occurring again. He recently researched and nominated five properties that have been successfully added to the National Register of Historic Places. He is the author of several recent history books including *Florida Prohibition: Corruption, Defiance and Tragedy* (The History Press, 2024). He also writes articles for historical journals, local newspapers and magazines and has appeared on several radio shows and PBS documentaries. He earned both a master's and a bachelor's degree from California State University.